40-DAY
Journey

WITH HOWARD THURMAN

40-Day Journey Series

Donna Schaper, Editor

Augsburg Books

Minneapolis

40-DAY JOURNEY WITH HOWARD THURMAN

Copyright © 2009 Augsburg Books, an imprint of Augsburg Fortress. All rights reserved. Except for brief quotations in critical articles or reviews, no part of this book may be reproduced in any manner without prior written permission from the publisher. Visit http://www.augsburgfortress.org/copyrights or write to Permissions, Augsburg Fortress, Box 1209, Minneapolis, MN 55440.

Unless otherwise identified, scripture quotations are from the New Revised Standard Version Bible, copyright © 1989 by the division of Christian Education of the National Council of the Churches of Christ in the USA. Used by permission. All rights reserved.

Daily readings from *Strange Freedom: The Best of Howard Thurman on Religious Experience and Public Life* by Walter Earl Fluker and Catherine Tumber. Copyright © 1998 by Walter Earl Fluker and Catherine Tumber. Reprinted by permission of Beacon Press, Boston.

Cover art: Photo by Olive Thurman Wong
Cover design: Laurie Ingram
Interior design: PerfecType, Nashville, Tenn.

Library of Congress Cataloging-in-Publication Data

40-day journey with Howard Thurman / Donna Schaper, editor.
    p. cm. — (The 40 day journey series)
  Includes bibliographical references and index.
  ISBN 978-0-8066-5769-1 (alk. paper)
  1. Spiritual journals—Authorship. 2. Spiritual exercises. 3. Devotional literature. 4. Spiritual life—Christianity.
5. Christian life—Baptist authors. 6. Thurman, Howard, 1900–1981. Strange freedom. I. Schaper, Donna.
II. Thurman, Howard, 1900–1981. Strange freedom. Selections. 2009. III. Title: Forty day journey with Howard Thurman.
  BV4509.5.A15 2009
  248.4'6—dc22
                              2009024841

The paper used in this publication meets the minimum requirements of American National Standard for Information Sciences—Permanence of Paper for Printed Library Materials, ANSI Z329.48-1984.

Printed in Canada

13   12   11   10   09   1   2   3   4   5   6   7   8   9   10

CONTENTS

Series Introduction

Imagine spending forty days with a great spiritual guide who has both the wisdom and the experience to help you along the path of your own spiritual journey. Imagine being able to listen to and question spiritual guides from the past and the present. Imagine being, as it were, mentored by women and men who have made their own spiritual journey and have recorded the landmarks, detours, bumps in the road, potholes, and wayside rests that they encountered along the way—all to help others (like you) who must make their own journey.

The various volumes in Augsburg Books' *40-Day Journey Series* are all designed to do just that—to lead you where your mind and heart and spirit long to go. As Augustine once wrote: *"You have made us for yourself, O Lord, and our heart is restless until it rests in you."* The wisdom you will find in the pages of this series of books will give you the spiritual tools and direction to find that rest. But there is nothing quietistic in the spirituality you will find here. Those who would guide you on this journey have learned that the heart that rests in God is one that lives with deeper awareness, deeper creativity, deeper energy, and deeper passion and commitment to the things that matter to God.

An ancient Chinese proverb states the obvious: the journey of a thousand miles begins with the first step. In a deep sense, books in the *40-Day Journey Series* are first steps on a journey that will not end when the forty days are over. No one can take the first step (or any step) for you.

Imagine that you are on the banks of the Colorado River. You are here to go white-water rafting for the first time and your guide has just described the experience, telling you with graphic detail what to expect. It sounds both exciting and frightening. You long for the experience but are somewhat disturbed, anxious, uncertain in the face of the danger that promises to accompany you on the journey down the river. The guide gets into the raft. She will accompany you on the journey, *but she can't take the journey for you.* If you want to experience the wildness of the river, the raw beauty of the canyon, the camaraderie of adventurers, and the mystery of a certain oneness with nature (and nature's creator), then you've got to get in the boat.

This book in your hand is like that. It describes the journey, provides a "raft," and invites you to get in. Along with readings from your spiritual guide, you will find scripture to mediate on, questions to ponder, suggestions for personal journaling, guidance in prayer, and a prayer for the day. If done faithfully each day, you will find the wisdom and encouragement you need to integrate meaningful spiritual insights and practices into your daily life. And when the 40-day journey is over it no longer will be the guide's description of the journey that stirs your longing for God but *your own experience* of the journey that grounds your faith and life and keeps you on the path.

I would encourage you to pick up other books in the series. There is only one destination, but many ways to get there. Not everything in every book will work for you (we are all unique), but in every book you will find much to help you discover your own path on the journey to the One in whom we all "live and move and have our being" (Acts 17:28).

May all be well with you on the journey.
Henry F. French, Series Editor

PREFACE

The work of Howard Thurman (1899–1981) is deep in a well-deserved
revival. Over thirteen doctoral dissertations have been written about his life
and work. Plans are afoot in Florida for a memorial. There are over fourteen
repositories of Howard Thurman's papers, with Boston University the largest
holding some 95% of his materials. The Quaker Retreat Center, Pendle Hill,
held a well-attended workshop last year on "Howard Thurman: In Search of
Genuine Community." A new multivolume work called *The Papers of Howard
Washington Thurman* is being published by the University of South Carolina
Press. This new collection includes correspondence in the 1950s between
Thurman and Dr. Martin Luther King Jr. And for my Christmas present two
years ago I requested and received his entire corpus of twenty-two books. It
has been my great pleasure to complete reading them.

In a time when racism and its possible demise is a subject on the minds
and hearts of many Americans, this black man who ministered in a segregated world has a story to tell. In a time when mysticism and social action
are enjoying a noisy divorce, Thurman is a model of the marriage of mysticism and social action worth noting. In a time when "moral values" have
once again been reduced to "private sexual behavior," Thurman's vigorous
and Christian defense and support of the "people whose backs are against the
wall" is a fine example of the marriage of religion and politics. Finally, in a
time when many announce with pride that they are not "religious but instead
spiritual," Thurman's own early development of a contagious ecumenical
spirituality puts him in the founder's seat.

Thurman's ecumenical spirituality was pioneering. Today we find it
normal for people to say they believe in God but don't go to church. When
Thurman first articulated a spirituality beyond institutional walls, he was
doing something new. He did not leave his past behind so much as bring

9

it into a contemporary context, taking its principles into foreign lands and unconvinced minds.

Thurman is also a great study right now because he has gone the way that the most recent American president has to go. He lived and succeeded in a multi-cultural world. He was equally the friend of blacks and whites. His Church for the Fellowship of All Peoples in California spoke of integration without the loss of racial or ethnic identity.

Thurman is fundamentally a religious man. His writing is fundamentally devotional. He enjoyed a faith that eschewed the demonization of others. He came from a small place and spent his life in large places. Widely scrutinized as a "first" at Boston University in the heart of the Brahmin North, he paved the way for literally hundreds of other integrationists. His ministry had many public outcomes but essentially was a mystical, pietistic and prayerful calling.

Many people wonder what would have happened to the large movements against racism and sexism in the 1960s if those movements had been more morally and spiritually grounded. Would it have been so easy for the religious right to box up the gospel in privatistic packages if the left had not become so secular and humanist? Would the staying power of people who hoped for more justice and more peace have been stronger if religious roots had been more respected? Thurman's life and ministry give us a way to look at these questions with both repentance and vigor. The best way to approach his work is through thoughtful devotional practice—and that is what this study encourages.

How to Use This Book

Your 40-day journey with Howard Thurman gives you the opportunity to be mentored by a great spiritual writer and Christian leader of the last century. The purpose of the journey, however, is not just to gain "head knowledge" about Howard Thurman. Rather, it is to begin living what you learn.

You will probably benefit most by fixing a special time of day in which to "meet with" your spiritual mentor. It is easier to maintain a spiritual practice if you do it regularly at the same time. For many people mornings, while the house is still quiet and before the busyness of the day begins, is a good time. Others will find that the noon hour or before bedtime serves well. We are all unique. Some of us are "morning people" and some of us are not. Do whatever works *for you* to maintain a regular meeting with Howard Thurman. Write it into your calendar and do your best to keep your appointments.

It is best if you complete your 40-day journey in forty days. A deepening focus and intensity of experience will be the result. However, it is certainly better to complete the journey than to give it up because you can't get it done in forty days. Indeed, making it a 40- or 20-week journey may better fit your schedule and it just might be that spending a whole week, or perhaps half a week, reflecting on the reading, the scripture, and the prayers, and then practicing what you are learning could be a powerfully transforming experience as well. Again, set a schedule that works for you, only be consistent.

Each day of the journey begins with a reading from Howard Thurman. You will note that the readings, from day to day, build on each other and introduce you to key ideas in his understanding of Christian life and faith. Read each selection slowly, letting the words sink into your consciousness. You may want to read each selection two or three times before moving on, perhaps reading it out loud once.

Following the reading from Howard Thurman's writings, you will find the heading *Biblical Wisdom* and a brief passage from the Bible that relates directly to what he has said. As with the selection from Thurman, read the biblical text slowly, letting the words sink into your consciousness.

Following the biblical reading, you will find the heading *Silence for Meditation.* Here you should take anywhere from five to twenty minutes meditating on the two readings. Begin by getting centered. Sit with your back straight, eyes closed, hands folded in your lap, and breathe slowly and deeply. Remember that breath is a gift of God; it is God's gift of life. Do nothing for two or three minutes other than simply observe your breath. Focus your awareness on the end of your nose. Feel the breath enter through your nostrils and leave through your nostrils. Once you feel your mind and spirit settling down, open your eyes and read both the daily reading and the biblical text again. Read them slowly, focus on each word or phrase, savor them, explore possible meanings and implications. At the end of each day you will find a blank section with the heading *Notes.* As you meditate on the readings, jot down any insights that occur to you. Do the readings raise any questions for you? Write them down. Do the readings suggest anything you should do? Write it down.

Stay at it as long as it feels useful. When your mind is ready to move on, close your eyes and observe your breath for a minute or so. Then return to the book and the next heading: *Questions to Ponder.* Here you will find a few pointed questions by Donna Schaper, the book's compiler and editor, on the day's reading. These are general questions intended for all spiritual seekers and communities of faith. Think them through and write your answers (and the implications of your answers for your own life of faith and for your community of faith) in the *Notes* section.

Many of these *Questions to Ponder* are designed to remind us—as Howard Thurman would affirm—that although spirituality is always personal, it is simultaneously relational and communal. A number of the questions, therefore, apply the relevance of the day's reading to faith communities. Just remember, a faith community may be as large as a regular organized gathering of any religious tradition, or as small as a family, or the relationship between spiritual friends. You don't need to be a member of a church, synagogue, mosque, or temple to be part of a faith community. Answer the questions in the context of your particular faith community.

Then move on to the heading *Psalm Fragment.* Here you will find a brief verse or two from the Hebrew book of Psalms that relate to the day's reading. The Psalms have always been the mainstay of prayer in the Christian tradition and always speak to the real situations in which we find ourselves—the kind of realism that Howard Thurman's work resonates with.

Reflect for a moment on the *Psalm Fragment* and then continue on to the heading *Journal Reflections.* Several suggestions for journaling are given that apply the readings to your own personal experience. It is in journaling that the "day" reaches its climax and the potential for transformative change is greatest. It would be best to buy a separate journal rather than use the *Notes* section of the book. For a journal you can use a spiral-bound or ring-bound notebook or one of the hardcover journal books sold in stationery stores. Below are some suggestions for how to keep a journal. For now, let's go back to the 40-day journey book.

The *Questions to Ponder* and *Journal Reflection* exercises are meant to assist you in reflecting on the daily reading and scripture quotations. Do not feel that you have to answer every question. You may choose which questions or exercises are most helpful to you. Sometimes a perfectly appropriate response to a question is, "I don't know" or "I'm not sure what I think about that." The important thing is to record your own thoughts and questions.

After *Journal Reflections*, you will find two more headings. The first is *Prayers of Hope & Healing*. One of the highest services a person of faith can perform is prayer for family and friends, for one's community of faith, for the victims of injustice, and for one's enemies. Under this heading you will find suggestions for prayer that relate to the key points in the day's readings. The last heading (before *Notes*) is *Prayer for Today*, a one or two line prayer to end your "appointment" with Howard Thurman, and to be prayed from time to time throughout the day.

Hints on Keeping a Journal

A journal is a very helpful tool. Keeping a journal is a form of meditation, a profound way of getting to know yourself—and God—more deeply. Although you could read your 40-day journey book and reflect on it "in your head," writing can help you focus your thoughts, clarify your thinking, and keep a record of your insights, questions, and prayers. Writing is generative: it enables you to have thoughts you would not otherwise have had.

A Few Hints for Journaling

1. Write in your journal with grace. Don't get stuck in trying to do it perfectly. Just write freely. Don't worry about literary style, spelling, or grammar. Your goal is simply to generate thoughts pertinent to your own life and get them down on paper.
2. You may want to begin and end your journaling with prayer. Ask for the guidance and wisdom of the Spirit (and thank God for that guidance and wisdom when you are done).
3. If your journaling takes you in directions that go beyond the journaling questions in your 40-day book, go there. Let the questions encourage, not limit, your writing.
4. Respond honestly. Don't write what you think you're supposed to believe. Write down what you really do believe, in so far as you can identify that. If you don't know, or are not sure, or if you have questions, record those. Questions are often openings to spiritual growth.
5. Carry your 40-day book and journal around with you every day during your journey (only keep them safe from prying eyes). The 40-day journey process is an intense experience that doesn't stop when you close the book. Your mind and heart and spirit will be engaged all day, and it will be helpful to have your book and journal handy to take notes or make new entries as they occur to you.

Journeying with Others

You can use your 40-day book with another person, a spiritual friend or partner, or with a small group. It would be best for each person first do his or her own reading, reflection, and writing in solitude. Then when you come together, share the insights you have gained from your time alone. Your discussion will probably focus on the *Questions to Ponder*, however, if the relationship is intimate, you may feel comfortable sharing some of what you have written in your journal. No one, however, should ever be pressured to share anything in their journal if they are not comfortable doing so.

Remember that your goal is to learn from one another, not to argue, nor to prove that you are right and the other person wrong. Just practice listening and trying to understand why your partner, friend, or colleague thinks as he or she does.

Practicing intercessory prayer together, you will find, will strengthen the spiritual bonds of those who take the journey together. And as you all work to translate insight into action, sharing your experience with each other is a way of encouraging and guiding each other and provides the opportunity to provide feedback to each other gently if that becomes necessary.

Continuing the Journey

When the forty days (or forty weeks) are over, a milestone has been reached, but the journey needn't end. One goal of the 40-day series is to introduce you to a particular spiritual guide with the hope that, having whet your appetite, you will want to keep the journey going. At the end of the book are some suggestions for further reading that will take you deeper on your journey with your mentor.

WHO IS HOWARD THURMAN?

How does a man who came from the nowhere of segregated Daytona Beach, Florida, still, years after his death, deserve to be a major figure in the somewhere of 21st century Christian thought and life? Clearly good luck, good mentoring, good parenting and a good mind joined up to create a uniquely fortunate man. He was the son of a father who died too soon. His mother, like most in his world, worked—and so did Howard.

His father, Saul Solomon Thurman, a big man with a large frame, worked on a railroad crew laying track for the Florida East Coast Rail from Jacksonville to Miami. He came home every two weeks. His grandmother—who did laundry and knew God—mostly raised Howard, whose job was to collect the soiled laundry and bring it home for her to wash. If there was another "parent" in this world it was the local Baptist church, which finally had its way with him. His conversion came young and surprised everyone in town with its intensity. The church had the sense to test it well and to support it early.

Once Mary McLeod Bethune's school choir sang at his church. Thurman was quite impressed with this African American educator and social activist's commitment to the education of Negro children. It was a building block in Thurman's developing understanding of and commitment to the importance of education for the Negro community. When Ms. Bethune died, it was Thurman's privilege to deliver her eulogy.

One piece of good luck and chance encounter stands out on Thurman's route to becoming a blessed man who could then bless others. By chance, Mr. James B. Gamble of the Union Trust Building, in Cincinnati, Ohio, one day asked Thurman to mail a letter for him. "Boy, "said Mr. Gamble, "you look like someone who could be trusted to mail these letters." Thurman made himself useful—and it was a major turning point in his life.

An influential relationship developed between Thurman and Gamble. He paid for Thurman to go to school, thus beginning the long road toward academic achievement of a bright but poor young man. Gamble paid $5.00 each month for Thurman's school fees and set him on his way to an education that has proved a very wise investment; it has benefited many.

Spiritual precocity joined with the Baptist Church, the luck of meeting James B. Gamble, and his grandmother and mother's fierce love and hope for him to create a boy who would become an important man. He was an early mystic, an almost empty vessel for the power of faith that was richly poured into him. Notably, his grandmother and mother "let him go" rather than hanging on to him. In his tribute to his grandmother at her death, Howard said, "I remember our silences."

When he finished his high school education, he went on to Morehouse College in Atlanta. His many letters home attest to the fact that money was often on his mind. He once was so worried about money that he skipped meals. Arriving home skinny and gaunt, his mother and his grandmother set him straight. Howard was to eat and not worry about them. He was, with their blessing, to get an education.

He consistently excelled in school because he preferred books to eating. Some would say he worked hard; I think he was simply in love with learning. There was a curiosity in him that was evident in his "fishing" expeditions as a child—the long nights he spent in a boat wondering what was going on in him and in the world, a curiosity that eventually would lead him to India and a visit with Mahatma Gandhi. The world was large to Thurman, and he increasingly saw himself as belonging deeply in it.

After graduating from Morehouse College in 1923, Thurman attended Colgate-Rochester Divinity School, where he graduated with a Bachelor of Divinity degree in 1925. It is interesting to note that he had originally applied to Andover Newton Theological Seminary but was turned down because he was Black. Thurman was ordained as a Baptist minister in 1925.

In 1932, Thurman accepted the position of professor of Christian theology in the Religion Department at Howard University in Washington, D.C., where he was later appointed Dean of Rankin Chapel.

In 1935, the national YMCA and YWCA International Committee, on behalf of the World Student Christian Federation, invited Thurman to be chairman of a four person Negro delegation to India, Ceylon, and Burma. On that trip Thurman met Gandhi and the two discussed Gandhi's criticism of Christianity as a religion that promoted segregation. As a result of that experience and Thurman's growing resolve to "make Christianity work for the weak as well as the strong," Thurman left Howard University in 1944 to co-found the Church for the Fellowship of All Peoples in San Francisco. The church deliberately drew together Whites, Blacks, Hispanics, and Asians in a thoroughly integrated congregation—the first such congregation in the United States.

At the Church for the Fellowship of All Peoples, Thurman modeled his theories of global ministry. Always an intellectual, he experimented with the arts and introduced dance as a sacred medium in the early 1950s. He pioneered a unique form of teaching in what was known as the "Intercultural Workshop," a methodology he used throughout his ministry and that was to be ably employed by many others as well.

In 1953, Thurman left California for Boston where he accepted the position of University Preacher and Professor of Spiritual Discipline and Resources at Boston University School of Theology. He was the first full-time Black dean at a White majority university in the United States.

Thurman married Kate Kelley in 1926; sadly she died of tuberculosis in 1930. Their daughter Olive (named after Olive Schreiner, the South African author, pacifist and political activist) came with him into his marriage to Sue E. Bailey in 1932. The couple had two children.

While Thurman was hardly a "race man"—a label that ordinarily means that race matters fundamentally to a person—he was also, by his own account, never unaware of color. Instead of being a race man he described himself as a "universalist." Within his profound global universalism, which comprehended caste and class as much as race, Thurman taught many how to see what was happening within what might be called the "community of the wall," the people who were outside and up against it consistently. Never unaware of race, he was also aware of much more.

In his writings, the language of "man" pervades and, while not a conscious obstacle for people when the books were written, today it can be experienced as exclusive. Thurman was not, however, unaware of the gifts of women, and although he used the language of his times, he understood the role and struggle of women who stood "with their backs against the wall.".

His broad, compassionate and inclusive spirit was probably more than a little early for its time. Once when he saw a store window advertising "Black Mammy and Pickanninies," Thurman invited the entire congregation to go stand in front of the store window and read it. The ad was removed. His emphasis on taking personal responsibility for social change began with himself and informed his leadership style.

He always lived on the other side of politics in mysticism, spirituality, prophecy, art, dancing, and hospitality. He combined the prophetic and mystical traditions of the Black church with an invitation to engage Jesus within the vicissitudes of contemporary life.

Thurman's liberating spirituality models a successful American approach to social action. Although the religious right might parody pragmatic social actions as "non spiritual," no such parody could be applied to Thurman. He begins mystically and spiritually and ends up politically, modeling the Jesus way to the "disinherited." In his book, *Jesus and the Disinherited*, he develops his theme of compassion and justice for those who stand with their backs against the wall. It has been reported that during the civil rights movement Dr. Martin Luther King, Jr. carried a copy of *Jesus and the Disinherited* wherever he went.

Thurman's more than twenty books show a profound link between spirituality and politics, mysticism and change, eternity and time, heaven and earth. Thurman is a bridge figure between rich and poor, compassionate and dispassionate, local and global, Black and White. His books built the bridges—those who read them are invited to walk across and meet in the middle.

(The editors of the anthology, *A Strange Freedom: The Best of Howard Thurman on Religious Experience and Public Life,* from which the Thurman readings in this book are taken, note that Thurman "did not use inclusive language with respect to gender;" however, they (and this book) have not altered his language in order "to preserve the lyrical flow of his prose.") I would like to thank Walter Earl Fluker, senior editor of the Howard Thurman Papers Project, for fact-checking this brief biography of Dr. Thurman.

40-DAY

Journey

WITH HOWARD THURMAN

Day 1

THERE ARE TWO REMARKABLE PICTURES given us by the Prophet Jeremiah (chapter 17). With these two pictures as a background, I want each of you to think seriously about this question: To what do I appeal when I want to convince myself that I am somebody?

First—a curse on him who relies on man, who depends upon mere human aid. For he is like a desert scrub that never thrives; set in a salt solitary place in the steppes—a striking picture! A certain kind of man likened unto a desert scrub—undeveloped and underdeveloped, undernourished and emaciated, stubby, and stunted, acting on the theory that to breathe is to live! What a character analysis!

He is thus, says Jeremiah, because he relies on man. He has a false sense of security. When such a man wants to convince himself that he is somebody, his appeal, most often, is to those things that are of temporary and passing significance.

I am putting the question quite personal[ly] this morning: In what do you find your security?"

~

BIBLICAL WISDOM

Cursed are those who trust in mere mortals and make mere flesh their strength . . . they shall be like a shrub in the desert, and shall not see when relief comes. Jeremiah 17: 5-6.

SILENCE FOR MEDITATION

QUESTIONS TO PONDER

- In what does your security lie?
- To what (or to whom) do you appeal when you want to convince yourself and others that you are somebody?
- Why is a "shrub in the desert" a good metaphor for people who rely on something less than God for security and a sense of self?

PSALM FRAGMENT

Be pleased, O God, to deliver me.
O LORD, make haste to help me! Psalm 70:1

JOURNAL REFLECTIONS

- Write a brief meditation on the ways you can (or cannot) be compared to a desert shrub.
- When you feel insecure, to what (or to whom) do you appeal to for security? Why?
- Is there anything going in your life from which you need deliverance? How might God be involved in that deliverance?

PRAYERS OF HOPE & HEALING

Pray both for your own security and for others who are also afraid. Pray that you and they would experience the truth that "there is no fear in love, but perfect love casts out fear" (1 John 4:18).

PRAYER FOR TODAY

When I feel like a shrub, O God, and about to blow away and be gone with the wind, secure me. Fasten me down to something lasting. Amen.

NOTES

Journey

Day 2

THE PROPHET (JEREMIAH 17:7-8) PICTURES the man who depends on God, who has God for his confidence, as a tree planted beside a stream sending his roots down to the water. He has no fear of scorching heat, his leaves are always green. He goes on bearing fruit when all around him is barren and lives serene. In other words such a man looks out on life with quiet eyes!

~

BIBLICAL WISDOM

Blessed are those who trust in the LORD,
*   whose trust is the LORD.*
They shall be like a tree planted by water,
*   sending out its roots by the stream.*
It shall not fear when heat comes,
*   and its leaves shall stay green;*
*   in the year of drought it is not anxious,*
*   and it does not cease to bear fruit.* Jeremiah 17:7-8

SILENCE FOR MEDITATION

QUESTIONS TO PONDER

- Does the metaphor of a "tree planted beside a stream" work for you as a picture of a person who has God for his or her confidence? Why or why not?
- Is it possible to live "serene" in a world like ours? If so, how? If not, why not?
- What do you think Thurman means when he talks about looking "out on life with quiet eyes"?

PSALM FRAGMENT

The LORD is my light and my salvation;
whom shall I fear?
The LORD is the stronghold of my life;
of whom shall I be afraid? Psalm 27:1

JOURNAL REFLECTIONS

- Write about whether or not (and why) you experience yourself as looking out on life with "quiet eyes."
- What other metaphors (besides a tree planted beside a stream) express for you a person whose confidence and trust is in God?
- Reflect on the spiritual disciplines you follow that help you to "live serene."

PRAYERS OF HOPE & HEALING

Pray for those who do not experience serenity in the face of our world's many problems, that they would learn to trust more deeply in the all-embracing grace of God.

PRAYER FOR TODAY

Gracious God, grant me quiet eyes to see the beauty of the earth, of the cosmos, of all that you have made, and especially grant me quiet eyes to see the beauty of my relationship with you. Amen.

NOTES

Day 3

GOD IS HERE. IN THE midst of life, breaking through the commonplace, glorifying the ordinary, the Great, High God is near. One should tread the earth with a deeply lying awe and reverence—God is in this place.

Do not wait to hear His spirit winging near in moments of great crisis, do not expect Him riding on the crest of a wave of deep emotional excitement—do not look to see Him at the dramatic moment when something abnormal or spectacular is at hand. Rather find Him in the simple experiences of daily living, in the normal ebb and flow of life as you live it.

↵

BIBLICAL WISDOM

Once Jesus was asked by the Pharisees when the kingdom of God was coming, and he answered, "The kingdom of God is not coming with things that can be observed; nor will they say, 'Look, here it is!' or 'There it is!' For, in fact, the kingdom of God is among you." Luke 17:20-21

SILENCE FOR MEDITATION

QUESTIONS TO PONDER

- Do you think more people look for God in extraordinary times and circumstances than in ordinary times and circumstances? Explain.
- In what ways does our culture encourage (or discourage) the experience of awe and reverence?
- How does your community of faith encourage (or discourage) the experience of awe and reverence?

Psalm Fragment

Where can I go from your spirit?
Or where can I flee from your presence?
If I ascend to heaven, you are there;
*   if I make my bed in Sheol, you are there.*
If I take the wings of the morning
*   and settle at the farthest limits of the sea,*
*   even there your hand shall lead me,*
*   and your right hand shall hold me fast.* Psalm 139:7-10

Journal Reflections

- Do you find God in the "normal ebb and flow of life as you live it"? Explain.
- Write about ways in which you have experienced God breaking through the commonplace and glorifying the ordinary.
- Write about times when you have experienced God's presence in extraordinary times and events. In what (if any) ways is the experience of God in the extraordinary different from the experience of God in the ordinary?

Prayers of Hope & Healing

Pray for people who seem to move through the day with no feelings of awe or reverence, that they may be opened to the everywhere presence of God.

Prayer for Today

God of great surprises, today let me find you in all the nooks and crannies of daily life. Amen.

Notes

Day 4

THE FINAL THING THAT MY faith teaches me is that God is love. Not only that He is; not only that he is near; but that he is love. Fully do I realize how difficult this is. There is so much anguish in life, so much misery unmerited, so much pain, so much downright reflective hell everywhere that it sometimes seems to me that it is an illusion to say that God is love. When one comes into close grips with the perversity of personalities, with studied evil—it might be forgiven one who cried aloud to the Power over Life—human life is stain—blot it out! I know all that. I know that this world is messed up and confused. I know that much of society stretches out like a gaping sore that refuses to be healed. I know that life is often heartless, hard as pig iron. And yet, in the midst of all this I affirm my faith that God is love—whatever else He might be.

BIBLICAL WISDOM

God is love, and those who abide in love abide in God, and God abides in them. 1 John 4:16

SILENCE FOR MEDITATION

QUESTIONS TO PONDER

- What about the realities of our world might lead someone to conclude that "it is an illusion to say that God is love"?
- What about the realities of our world might lead someone to conclude that God is love?
- How does faith that God is love shape one's perspective on the realities of the world?

PSALM FRAGMENT

Prove me, O LORD, and try me;
*   test my heart and mind.*
For your steadfast love is before my eyes,
*   and I walk in faithfulness to you.* Psalm 26:2-3

JOURNAL REFLECTIONS

- Do you find it easy or difficult to believe that God is love? Explain.
- If you believe that God is love, how do you account for evil and suffering?
- If you believe that God is love, how does that belief help shape the way you make the decisions that get you from morning to night?

PRAYERS OF HOPE & HEALING

Pray for those whose lives lack the give and take of love, that somehow love would enter their lives.

PRAYER FOR TODAY

God of love, this day let me follow you by loving. Amen.

NOTES

Day 5

IT WAS THE YEAR OF Halley's comet. I was a little boy living in a sawmill town in Florida. I had not seen the comet in the sky because my mother made me go to bed with the setting of the sun. Some of my friends who were more privileged had tried to convey to me their impression of the awe-inspiring spectacle. And I heard my stepfather say one day when he came home for lunch that a man had been down at the mill office selling what he called "comet pills." The theory was that if these pills were taken according to directions, when the tail of the comet struck the earth the individual would be immune. As I remember it, the owner of the saw-mill made several purchases, not only for himself and family, but also for his key workmen—the idea being that after the debacle he would be able to start business over again.

⌒

BIBLICAL WISDOM

Therefore I tell you, do not worry about your life, what you will eat or what you will drink, or about your body, what you will wear. Is not life more than food, and the body more than clothing? Look at the birds of the air; they neither sow nor reap nor gather into barns, and yet your heavenly Father feeds them. Are you not of more value than they? And can any of you by worrying add a single hour to your span of life? Matthew 6:25-27

SILENCE FOR MEDITATION

QUESTIONS TO PONDER

- How would you describe the metaphorical meaning of "comet pills?"
- In what ways does our culture encourage us to buy "comet pills" in order to protect ourselves against the dangers—real or imagined—of life?
- How might a community of faith lessen the allure of "comet pills?"

Psalm Fragment

Call on me in the day of trouble;
I will deliver you, and you shall glorify me. Psalm 50:15

Journal Reflections

- Do you find the idea of "comet pills" funny or disturbing or both? Explain.
- Make a list of the "comet pills" you have been tempted to try. Which (if any) did you try? In what ways did they (or did they not) allay your anxiety or solve your problem?
- Have you ever treated God as a "comet pill"? Have you ever found God replacing the need for "comet pills"? Explain.

Prayers of Hope & Healing

Pray for those who are addicted to "comet pills," that they might experience the liberating wonder of trust in God's mercy and love.

Prayer for Today

God, on this day, the stars will come out and comets may even fly about. Grant me the grace to really see them and to see you as the source of their being and beauty. Amen.

Notes

Day 6

ONE NIGHT I WAS AWAKENED by my mother, who asked if I would like to see the comet. I got up, dressed quickly, and went out with her into the back yard. There I saw in the heavens the awesome tail of the comet and stood transfixed. With deep anxiety I asked, without taking my eyes off it, "What will happen to us when that thing falls out of the sky?" There was a long silence during which I felt the gentle pressure of her fingers on my shoulders; then I looked into her face and saw what I had seen on another occasion, when without knocking I had rushed into her room and found her in prayer. At last she said, "Nothing will happen to us, Howard. God will take care of us." In that moment something was touched and kindled in me, a quiet reassurance that has never quite deserted me. As I look back on it, what I sensed then was the fact that what stirred in me was one with what created and controlled the comet. It was this inarticulate awareness that silenced my fear and stilled my panic.

❧

BIBLICAL WISDOM

By this we know that we abide in him and he in us, because he has given us of his Spirit. 1 John 4:13

SILENCE FOR MEDITATION

QUESTIONS TO PONDER

- The comet can be seen as a metaphor for the many dangers life places in our way. In what ways does faith give you a unique perspective on those dangers?
- Does it seem realistic or naïve to say, like Mrs. Thurman, "God will take care of us" when faced with danger? Explain.

- Thurman wrote that while watching the comet he realized that what stirred in him "was one with what created and controlled the comet." In what ways might the sense of God's indwelling presence help us to face our fears?

PSALM FRAGMENT

By the word of the LORD the heavens were made,
and all their host by the breath of his mouth.
The LORD looks down from heaven;
he sees all humankind.
From where he sits enthroned he watches
all the inhabitants of the earth—
he who fashions the hearts of them all,
and observes all their deeds. Psalm 33:6, 13-15

JOURNAL REFLECTIONS

- Write about a time when you were afraid. Were you delivered from fear? If so, how? If not, how do you go on in spite of your fear?
- When you are afraid, where (or to whom) do you turn for comfort? Why turn there?
- Write about a time when you were a source of comfort for another who was afraid. What did you do or say? How did things turn out?

PRAYERS OF HOPE & HEALING

Pray for those who are afraid, that they would find comfort and courage in God and in their community of faith. Pray for those who give comfort and courage to others, that they would experience God's love in their love.

PRAYER FOR TODAY

Loving God, let me take comfort and courage from the experience of your love and let me give comfort and courage to others as an expression of your love. Amen.

NOTES

MANY AND VARIED ARE THE interpretations dealing with the teachings and life of Jesus of Nazareth. But few of these interpretations deal with what the teachings and life of Jesus have to say to those who stand, at a moment in human history, with their backs against the wall.

To those who need profound succor and strength to enable them to live in the present with dignity and creativity, Christianity often has been sterile and of little avail. The conventional Christian word is muffled, confused, and vague. Too often the price exacted by society for security and respectability is that the Christian movement in its formal expression must be on the side of the strong against the weak. This is a matter of tremendous significance, for it reveals to what extent a religion that was born of a people acquainted with persecution and suffering has become the cornerstone of a civilization and of nations whose very position in modern life has too often been secured by a ruthless use of power applied to weak and defenseless people.

⟶

BIBLICAL WISDOM

"The Spirit of the Lord is upon me,
because he has anointed me
to bring good news to the poor.
He has sent me to proclaim release to the captives
and recovery of sight to the blind,
to let the oppressed go free,
to proclaim the year of the Lord's favor." Luke 4:18-19

SILENCE FOR MEDITATION

QUESTIONS TO PONDER

- Do you agree or disagree with Thurman's critique of the church? Why?
- How would you summarize the teachings and life of Jesus of Nazareth?
- Why is it that the "conventional Christian word" might be experienced by those who suffer from social injustice and oppression as "sterile and of little avail"?

PSALM FRAGMENT

For the needy shall not always be forgotten,
nor the hope of the poor perish forever.
Rise up, O LORD! Do not let mortals prevail;
let the nations be judged before you. Psalm 9:18-19

JOURNAL REFLECTIONS

- Have you or someone you know ever stood with your back "against the wall"? If so, was the teaching and practice of the church a source of comfort and strength or not? Explain.
- In your experience, do the way of Jesus and the way of the church seem to be the same or different? Explain.
- In what ways does the church support you in following Jesus? In what ways does your following of Jesus critique the church?

PRAYERS OF HOPE & HEALING

Pray for the church, that it may constantly and humbly wonder if it is faithfully following the way of Jesus, which is the way of love and justice.

PRAYER FOR TODAY

Loving God, let me be faithful in living like Jesus, "the way, the truth, and the life." Amen.

NOTES

Day 8

THE MYSTERY OF LIFE AND death persists despite the exhaustless and exhaustive treatment it has been given in song and story, philosophy and science, in art and religion. The human spirit is so involved in the endless cycle of birth, of living and dying, that in some sense each man is an authority, a key interpreter of the meaning of the totality of the experience. The testimony of the individual, then, is always fresh if he is able to make himself articulate to his fellows. Even when he is not, there is the persistent conviction that in some profound sense he himself knows and understands. When the external circumstances of life are dramatic or unusual, causing the human spirit to make demands upon all the reaches of its resourcefulness in order to keep from being engulfed, then the value of its findings made articulate, has more than passing significance.

BIBLICAL WISDOM

For everything there is a season, and a time for every matter under heaven:
  a time to be born, and a time to die;
  a time to plant, and a time to pluck up what is planted. . . . Ecclesiastes 3:1-2

SILENCE FOR MEDITATION

QUESTIONS TO PONDER

- In what sense is each person "an authority" on the experience of living and dying?
- In what ways does religious faith help us address the "mystery of life and death"?
- What attitudes might you expect to find in people who accept life and death as mysteries to be lived in rather than as problems to be explained and solved?

PSALM FRAGMENT

Bless the LORD, O my soul,
*   and do not forget all his benefits—*
who forgives all your iniquity,
who heals all your diseases,
who redeems your life from the Pit,
who crowns you with steadfast love and mercy. . . . Psalm 103:2-4

JOURNAL REFLECTIONS

- Write a brief meditation on how you understand the mystery of your own life and your own death at this present moment.
- Reflect on any experiences you have had that confronted you with the reality of death. What did you learn?
- Write about the relationship between being ready to die and being ready to live. Are you ready? For both? Explain.

PRAYERS OF HOPE & HEALING

Pray for those who are dying or afraid of death, that they might find courage through faith in the author of life. Pray for all who "walk through the darkest valley," that they would "fear no evil" for God is with them.

PRAYER FOR TODAY

God of salvation, let me celebrate my life today, knowing that death can never separate me from your love. Amen.

NOTES

Journey

Day 9

DEATH WAS A FACT, INESCAPABLE, persistent. For the slave, it was extremely compelling because of the cheapness with which his life was regarded. The slave was a tool, a thing, a utility, a commodity, but he was not a *person*. He was faced constantly with the imminent threat of death, of which the terrible overseer was the symbol; and the awareness that he (the slave) was only chattel property, the dramatization. . . . If a slave were killed, it was merely a property loss, a matter of bookkeeping. The notion of personality, of human beings as ends so basic to the genius of the Christian faith, had no authentic application in the relationship between slave and master. The social and religious climate were uncongenial to such an ethic.

~

BIBLICAL WISDOM

(Paul, on returning the slave Onesimus to his master, Philemon) *I wanted to keep him with me . . . but I preferred to do nothing without your consent, in order that your good deed might be voluntary and not something forced. Perhaps this is the reason he was separated from you for a while, so that you might have him back forever, no longer as a slave but more than a slave, a beloved brother— especially to me but how much more to you, both in the flesh and in the Lord.* Philemon 1:13-16

SILENCE FOR MEDITATION

QUESTIONS TO PONDER

- List some of the ways our culture condones treating others as "a tool, a thing, a utility, a commodity."
- In what ways, if any, have Christian churches allowed an ethic that is contradictory to the ethic of Christ?
- In what ways is our social and religious climate congenial or uncongenial to an ethic that sees each human being as an end and not simply a means for others to use?

PSALM FRAGMENT

How very good and pleasant it is
when kindred live together in unity! . . .
For there the LORD ordained his blessing,
life forevermore. Psalm 133:1, 3b

JOURNAL REFLECTIONS

- Have you ever felt like "a tool, a thing, a utility, a commodity"? If so, describe the experience. If not, can you imagine being treated that way and feeling that way?
- How does your faith shape the way you relate to other people?
- Reflect on what it must be like to be "faced constantly with the threat of death." Where could you find hope? Meaning? Dignity?

PRAYERS OF HOPE & HEALING

Pray for those who lives are damaged by discrimination of any kind, that they might find true fellowship, true welcome and acceptance, true community. Pray for those who discriminate against others, that they might have the grace to see that we are all brothers and sisters, children of the same Father, beloved of God and worthy of respect and care and dignity.

PRAYER FOR TODAY

Compassionate God, this day, let me show the hospitality, the acceptance, the kindness, care, and compassion that are signs of your kingdom. Amen.

NOTES

Journey

Day 10

(IN THE NEGRO SPIRITUALS) LIFE is regarded as a pilgrimage, a sojourn, while the true home of the spirit is beyond the vicissitudes of life with God! This is a familiar theme of the human spirit. We are dealing with a striking theory of time. Time is measured in terms of events, actions, therefore intentions and desires. All experience, then, is made up of a series of more or less intense meaning-units that may fall in such rapid succession that the interval between is less than any quantitative value. Within the scope of an event-series all of human life is bound. Freedom can only mean, in this sense, the possibility of release from the tyranny of succeeding intervals of events. The totality of life then, in its existential aspects, is thus completely exhausted in time. Death in such a view means complete cessation of any sense of interval and therefore of any sense of events. In short, here death means either finality or complete absorption from time-space awareness. Whatever transpires beyond death, while it can be thought of only in terms of time-space intervals, is of another universe of discourse, another quality of being.

ↄ

BIBLICAL WISDOM

They confessed that they were strangers and foreigners on the earth, for people who speak in this way make it clear that they are seeking a homeland. If they had been thinking of the land that they had left behind, they would have had opportunity to return. But as it is, they desire a better country, that is, a heavenly one. Therefore God is not ashamed to be called their God; indeed, he has prepared a city for them. Hebrews 11:13b-16

SILENCE FOR MEDITATION

QUESTIONS TO PONDER

- The Negro spirituals saw life as a "pilgrimage," a journey of faith through life and death toward God. Do you agree? Why or why not?

- What's more important, the journey or the destination? Or are they equally important? Explain.
- If freedom means the "possibility of release from the tyranny of succeeding intervals of events," how is it possible to experience freedom on this side of death?

PSALM FRAGMENT

My vows to you I must perform, O God;
I will render thank offerings to you.
For you have delivered my soul from death,
and my feet from falling,
so that I may walk before God
in the light of life. Psalm 56:12-13

JOURNAL REFLECTIONS

- Write a brief meditation describing your life as a pilgrimage. From where are you coming; to where are you going? Through what landscapes are you journeying? Where is God on your journey?
- What in your present experience are the events, actions, intentions and desires that measure time for you? Are they freeing or enslaving?
- Do you experience the flow of time as "tyranny" or "freedom"? Explain.

PRAYERS OF HOPE & HEALING

Pray for those for whom life's journey is marked by suffering and fear, that they might experience the freedom of the children of God. Pray for all people, that their individual journeys might take them deeper into wisdom, deeper into God.

PRAYER FOR TODAY

God of time and eternity, today let me walk beside you as I journey toward you. Amen.

NOTES

Journey

Day 11

SUFFERING IS UNIVERSAL FOR MANKIND. There is no one who escapes. It makes demands alike upon the wise and the foolish, the literate and the illiterate, the saint and the sinner. Very likely it bears no relationship to the character of the individual; it often cannot be assessed in terms of merit or demerit, reward or punishment. Men have tried to build all kinds of immunities against it. Much of the meaning of all human striving is to be found in the desperate effort of the spirit of man to build effective windbreaks against the storm of pain that sweeps across the human path. Man has explored the natural world around him, the heights and depths of his own creative powers, the cumulative religious experience of the race—all in an effort to find some means of escape, but no escape is to be found. Suffering stalks man, never losing the scent, and soon or late seizes upon him to wreak its devastation.

◡

BIBLICAL WISDOM

Rejoice in hope, be patient in suffering, persevere in prayer. Romans 12:12

SILENCE FOR MEDITATION

QUESTIONS TO PONDER

- Are there any immunities against suffering? Explain.
- In what ways might the fact of our suffering be experienced as shame?
- How (for good or for ill) might suffering impact our experience of God?

PSALM FRAGMENT

In you, O Lord, I take refuge;
let me never be put to shame. Psalm 71:1

JOURNAL REFLECTIONS

- Write about a time when you experienced great physical, emotional, psychological, or spiritual suffering. How did the experience affect your faith?
- Where was God in your suffering?
- What did suffering teach you?

PRAYERS OF HOPE & HEALING

Pray for those who suffer for any reason, that in their suffering they might experience the healing, comforting presence of God. Pray that they might find themselves surrounded by a loving and caring community of faith.

PRAYER FOR TODAY

God of great compassion, when I suffer please remind me that nothing—not even my suffering—can separate me from your love. Amen.

NOTES

Day 12

To Jesus, God was Creator of life and the living substance, the Living Stream upon which all things moved, the Mind containing time, space, and all their multitudinous offspring. And beyond all these, He was Friend and Father. The time most precious for the Master was at close of day. This was the time for the long breath, when all the fragments left by the commonplace, all the little hurts and big aches, came to rest; when the mind could be freed of the immediate demand, and voices that had been stilled by the long day's work could once more be heard; when there could be the deep sharing of innermost secrets and the laying bare of heart and mind—yes, the time most precious for him was at close of day.

BIBLICAL WISDOM

Immediately he made the disciples get into the boat and go on ahead to the other side, while he dismissed the crowds. And after he had dismissed the crowds, he went up the mountain by himself to pray. When evening came, he was there alone. . . . Matthew 14:22-23

SILENCE FOR MEDITATION

QUESTIONS TO PONDER

- What do you think Thurman means by "the time for the long breath"?
- In what ways does our culture discourage us from taking the time for the long breath?
- Does your community of faith encourage people and train them to take regular time for prayer and meditation? Explain.

PSALM FRAGMENT

I commune with my heart in the night;
  I meditate and search my spirit. . . . Psalm 77:6

Journal Reflections

- Thurman describes God as "Creator of life and the Living Substance, the Living Stream upon which all things moved, the Mind containing time, space, and all their multitudinous offspring." He also calls God "Friend and Father." Do these images work for you? Why or why not?
- If someone asked you to describe God, what images would you use? Why?
- Describe the spiritual practices you follow that help you take the "long breath." Anything you're not doing that you would like to try? How could you get started?

Prayers of Hope & Healing

Pray for those who don't take the "long breath," that they might discover its healing, strengthening power. Pray for those who do take the "long breath," that they might share their practice with others.

Prayer for Today

Loving God, today let me breathe deeply, let me take time to be still and alone with you; come and surprise me with your precious presence. Amen.

Notes

Journey

Day 13

THERE IS AN ELEMENT OF profound truth in the outlook of pantheism, which sees the work of God in the world of nature with such clarity as to identify God with His world; the temptation is hard to resist. But this is not enough. God must never be a prisoner in His creation. When I look carefully at my own body, I see at once that my body functions are so closely meshed and integrated that, under ordinary circumstances, I am not aware of any part of my body as such unless the inner harmony breaks down at the point of function. I do not become little finger aware unless my little finger no longer functions as a little finger should. When the harmony is broken, I say that the part is ill or the body is ill. The body is quite literally a dwelling place of the Most High God, Creator of the Universe. The mood of reverence applies here with telling effect upon man's whole world of values, meaning, and morality.

⁓

BIBLICAL WISDOM

For we are the temple of the living God; as God said,
  "I will live in them and walk among them,
  and I will be their God,
  and they shall be my people." 2 Corinthians 6:16

SILENCE FOR MEDITATION

QUESTIONS TO PONDER

- What does it mean to say that "God must never be a prisoner in His creation"?
- What can you learn about God by paying attention to the natural world?
- What are the moral implications of affirming that "the body is quite literally a dwelling place of the Most High God, Creator of the Universe"?

PSALM FRAGMENT

Let the heavens be glad, and let the earth rejoice;
let the sea roar, and all that fills it;
let the field exult, and everything in it.
Then shall all the trees of the forest sing for joy
before the LORD. Psalm 96:11-13b

JOURNAL REFLECTIONS

- If you have had such experiences, write about times when you have felt God dwelling within you.
- If you have a sense of the indwelling presence of God, how does that influence the way you live? How does it affect your relationships?
- Does your experience of God create in you an increased reverence for all life? Explain.

PRAYERS OF HOPE & HEALING

Pray for those who do not sense God present with and within them, that they might experience the wonder of their bodies as temples of God.

PRAYER FOR TODAY

Holy Spirit, teach me to treasure my body and the bodies of others as your temple. Teach me to approach the harmony of body and spirit with reverence. Amen.

NOTES

Journey

Day 14

ONE OF THESE (SPIRITUAL PRACTICES) is the practice of silence, or quiet. As a child I was accustomed to spend many hours alone in my rowboat, fishing along the river, where there was no sound save the lapping of the waves against the boat. There were times when it seemed as if the earth and the river and the sky and I were one beat of the same pulse. It was a time of watching and waiting for what I did not know—yet I always knew. There would come a moment when beyond the single pulse beat there was a sense of Presence which seemed always to speak to me. My response to the sense of Presence always had the quality of personal communion. There was no voice. There was no image. There was no vision. There was God.

~

BIBLICAL WISDOM

Be still, and know that I am God. Psalm 46:10

SILENCE FOR MEDITATION

QUESTIONS TO PONDER

- Sometimes the noise inside is almost as bad as the noise outside. How can you escape all the noise and enter into stillness and silence?
- What is the significance of the fact that Thurman calls "silence" and "quiet" a "practice"?
- What role does silence have (if any) in the worship of your faith community?

PSALM FRAGMENT

For God alone my soul waits in silence,
for my hope is from him.
He alone is my rock and my salvation,
my fortress; I shall not be shaken. Psalm 62:5-6

JOURNAL REFLECTIONS

- Do you feel drawn to stillness, silence, solitude or are you repelled by them? Explain.
- Thurman speaks of feeling a oneness with all of nature. Do you ever feel that way? If so, in what ways? If not, can you imagine such a feeling?
- Thurman speaks of a "sense of Presence" emerging from his experience of oneness with nature. Write about places and times and circumstances when you have had a "sense of Presence."

PRAYERS OF HOPE & HEALING

Pray for those for whom the natural world is not a window on the divine, that they might learn to see the Creator in the creation. Amen.

PRAYER FOR TODAY

Holy God, let me find the time to be still today and know you in the stillness. Let me experience the silence in which your love speaks in the midst of a noisy world. Amen.

NOTES

Journey

Day 15

MANY YEARS AFTER, I WAS invited to speak at a Friends First Day Meeting in Pennsylvania. I decided to put aside my usual procedures of preparation for an address and expose myself completely and utterly to the time of "centering down" in the Quaker meeting. I felt that if I were able to share profoundly in that clarifying, centering process the word to be spoken would be clear and sure. I was accustomed to quiet and silence in private but not as part of a collective experience, and I entered into it with some trepidation. After a while all the outer edges of my mind and spirit began to move toward the center. As a matter of fact, the movement seemed to me to be actually fluid and flowing. After some time, I am not sure precisely when, the sense of the movement of my spirit disappeared and a great living stillness engulfed me. And then a strange thing happened. There came into my mind, as if on a screen, first a single word and then more words, until there was in my mind's eye an entire sentence from the Sermon on the Mount. The curious thing was that, familiar as I was with the passage, one part of my mind waited for each word to appear as the sentence built, while another part knew what the sentence was going to say. When it was all there, with avidity my mind seized upon it. I began thinking about it as the text of what I would say.

↵

BIBLICAL WISDOM

Blessed are the poor in spirit, for theirs is the kingdom of God. Matthew 5:3

SILENCE FOR MEDITATION

QUESTIONS TO PONDER

- There is such a thing as improvisation and there is such a thing as inspiration. What is the difference?

- Thurman speaks of the "clarifying, centering process " of the Quaker meeting. How does your community of faith discern what God might be saying to you?
- Is your faith community open or closed to people sharing experiences such as Thurman points to in today's reading? Explain.

PSALM FRAGMENT

Let me hear what God the LORD will speak,
  for he will speak peace to his people,
    to his faithful, to those who turn to him in their hearts. Psalm 85:8

JOURNAL REFLECTIONS

- Does Thurman's experience at the Quaker meeting resonate with you? Why or why not?
- Describe the practices you follow to "center down." If you don't know how to get centered, who could you talk to in order to learn?
- Describe a time when you felt as if God were speaking to you. How did you know it was God? What did you learn? How did it impact your life?

PRAYERS OF HOPE & HEALING

Pray for those who are so distracted by the cares and worries of the world that they cannot center down and tend to God, that they might find ways of entering the silence where the God who is love speaks.

PRAYER FOR TODAY

Create in me a clean heart, O God, and put a new and right spirit within me. . . . Restore to me the joy of your salvation, and sustain in me a willing spirit. Amen (Psalm 51:10-12).

NOTES

Day 16

ONCE THE INTERFERENCE THAT DROWNS out the hunger has been stilled or removed, real communion between man and God can begin. Slowly the hunger begins to stir until it moves inside the individual's self-consciousness, and the sense of the very Presence of God becomes manifest. The words that are uttered, if there be words, may be halting and poor; they may have to do with some deep and searching need of which the individual now becomes acutely aware; it may be a sin that had become so much a part of the landscape of the soul that the soul itself has the feeling of corruption—but this may not last long. On the other hand, it may be a rather swift outpouring of a concern, because here is the moment of complete understanding and the freedom it inspires.

BIBLICAL WISDOM

Blessed are those who hunger and thirst for righteousness, for they will be filled.
Matthew 5: 6

SILENCE FOR MEDITATION

QUESTIONS TO PONDER

- What is the "hunger" about which Thurman writes?
- What evidence for this hunger do you find in the church, in society, in yourself?
- What kinds of "interference" drown out the hunger? In other words, for what besides God do people hunger and thirst? In what ways might the interference be lessened or eliminated?

PSALM FRAGMENT

O God, you are my God, I seek you,
  my soul thirsts for you;
  my flesh faints for you,
  as in a dry and weary land where there is no water. Psalm 63:1

JOURNAL REFLECTIONS

- Thurman writes that: "Slowly the hunger begins to stir until it moves inside the individual's self-consciousness, and the sense of the very Presence of God becomes manifest." If you have had such an experience, write about it in your journal.
- At times when you have been deeply aware of the presence of God, what, if any, needs and concerns arose from the experience? What did you say to God? Ask from God?
- Describe in your journal the spiritual practices you follow that answer to your hunger for God.

PRAYERS OF HOPE & HEALING

Pray for those whose hunger for God is drowned out by the distractions, cares and concerns of the world, that they might break through and encounter God within them.

PRAYER FOR TODAY

O God, let me feel my spiritual hunger with joy and be willing to be fed. Amen.

NOTES

Journey

Day 17

SEVERAL YEARS AGO I WAS talking with a very old lady about prayer, and particularly her own experience in prayer. She told me a story from her own most recent past. In her little Congregational church in a small New England community there was an extended crisis over the minister. The congregation felt he should leave because his usefulness was over. He prayed about the matter and as a result was convinced that, all evidence to the contrary notwithstanding, he should remain at his post. My friend said that she decided to take the matter directly to God in her prayer time. I quote her:

> I gave myself plenty of time. I went into a thorough review of the highlights of the sixty years I have been a member of the church right up to the present situation. I talked it through very carefully. It was so good to talk freely and to know that the feelings and the thoughts behind the words were being understood. When I finished I said, "Now Father, these are the facts as best I can state them. Take them and do the best you can. I have no suggestions to make."

A fresh meaning flooded the words "Thy Will be done."

⌁

BIBLICAL WISDOM

Your kingdom come.
Your will be done,
    on earth as it is in heaven. Matthew 6:10

SILENCE FOR MEDITATION

QUESTIONS TO PONDER

- Do you find it easy to talk to others about prayer and your experience in prayer? Why or why not?
- Does the idea of prayer as simply talking things through make sense to you? Why or why not?

- Does praying to God about a problem without offering God suggestions as to what to do about it make sense to you? Why or why not?

PSALM FRAGMENT

I wait for the LORD, my soul waits,
and in his word I hope;
my soul waits for the Lord
more than those who watch for the morning,
more than those who watch for the morning. Psalm 130:5-6

- Write about a time when you used prayer—a conversation with God—to review a situation or problem that was troubling you. Was it helpful? Why or why not?
- What would it mean to you to say, "My soul waits for the Lord"?
- Is it easy or difficult for you to speak with God about some problem or circumstance and not offer suggestions as to what God should do? Explain.

PRAYERS OF HOPE & HEALING

Pray for those faced with difficult decisions or troubling circumstances, that they may have the grace to talk things through with God and then wait on God for direction.

PRAYER FOR TODAY

Listening God, this day let me talk about everything with you and let me spend at least as much time listening as talking. Amen.

NOTES

Day 18

Communion may be an overflowing of utter praise, adoration, and celebration. The sense of awe becomes trumpet-tongued, and the sheer joy of the beauty of holiness overwhelms the mind and enlivens all the emotions with a kindling of spiritual fervor. It is at such a moment that one feels he was created to praise God and to enjoy Him forever.

The communion may be an overflowing of thanksgiving. Here I do not mean an order of thanks for services rendered or for good received. Here is no perfunctory grace before meals, when a person chooses to mumble gratitude either out of habit, or superstition, or because of spiritual breeding of a high order. No, I do not mean this sort of thing, but rather the overflowing of the heart as an act of grace toward God. The overflow is not merely because of what has taken place in life or in the world or because of all the manifestations of benevolence that have covered a life.

*

Biblical Wisdom

Rejoice always, pray without ceasing, give thanks in all circumstances; for this is the will of God in Christ Jesus for you. 1 Thessalonians 5:16-18

Silence for Meditation

Questions to Ponder

- Thurman describes communion with God as "an overflowing of utter praise, adoration, and celebration," and as "an overflowing of thanksgiving." Is his description supported by your own experience? Explain.
- What words might you use to describe the experience of communion with God?
- In what ways does worship in your community of faith encourage (or perhaps discourage) your experience of communion with the divine?

PSALM FRAGMENT

O come, let us sing to the LORD;
*   let us make a joyful noise to the rock of our salvation!*
Let us come into his presence with thanksgiving;
*   let us make a joyful noise to him with songs of praise!*
O come, let us worship and bow down,
*   let us kneel before the LORD, our Maker!* Psalm 95:1-2, 6

JOURNAL REFLECTIONS

- Write about an experience of "spiritual fervor." What "kindled" the experience? What impact did it have on you?
- Reflect on "thanksgiving" as a state of being rather than as simple gratitude for something received or done for you.
- Does thanksgiving describe your way of being in the world? Explain.

PRAYERS OF HOPE & HEALING

Pray for those for whom life lacks passion, that they might have kindled within them the fire of divine love.

PRAYER FOR TODAY

This day, O God, let me be afire with passion for you and the world you love. Amen.

NOTES

Day 19

THERE IS A STRANGE NECESSITY in the human spirit that a man deal with his sin before God. This necessity is honored in prayer when the deed is laid bare and the guilt acknowledged. I do not know how it happens or quite how to describe it, but I do know that again and again man has come away from prayer freed of his guilt, and with his sin forgiven; he then has a sense of being totally understood, completely dealt with, thoroughly experienced, and utterly healed. This is not to suggest that after the experience a man is always through with his sin. No, but now a solvent is at work on it which dissolves it, and the virus begins to be checked in its breeding place.

BIBLICAL WISDOM

If we say that we have no sin, we deceive ourselves, and the truth is not in us. If we confess our sins, he who is faithful and just will forgive us our sins and cleanse us from all unrighteousness. 1 John 1:8-9

SILENCE FOR MEDITATION

QUESTIONS TO PONDER

- Our culture (and many of our churches) does not like to talk about sin. Why do you think that is so?
- Do you agree that there is "a strange necessity in the human spirit" that moves us to deal with our sin before God? Explain.
- Thurman says that when we deal with our sin before God and experience forgiveness "a solvent" goes to work on our sin dissolving it. Has that been your experience? Explain.

PSALM FRAGMENT

Happy are those whose transgression is forgiven,
whose sin is covered. . . .
While I kept silence, my body wasted away
through my groaning all day long. . . .
Then I acknowledged my sin to you,
and I did not hide my iniquity;
I said, "I will confess my transgressions to the LORD,"
and you forgave the guilt of my sin. Psalm 32:1,3,5

JOURNAL REFLECTIONS

- Write about your understanding and experience of the cycle of sin, repentance, confession, and forgiveness.
- When you are honest with God about your sin, do you come away with "a sense of being totally understood, completely dealt with, thoroughly experienced, and utterly healed"? If yes, write about the experience. If no, how do you come away from the experience of bringing your sin to God?
- St. Paul told Christians: "Consider yourselves dead to sin and alive to God in Christ Jesus" (Romans 6:11). What would it mean to you to do just that?

PRAYERS OF HOPE & HEALING

Pray for all who need healing in body, mind, or spirit, that they would bring their need to God and experience the healing, comforting power of Holy Spirit.

PRAYER FOR TODAY

Forgiving God, today let me be honest with you about myself and, when necessary, let me ask for, receive and live in your forgiveness. Amen.

NOTES

Day 20

THE EXPERIENCE OF PRAYER, AS I have been describing it, can be nurtured and cultivated. It can create a climate in which a man's life moves and functions. Indeed, it may become a way of living for the individual. It is ever possible that the time may come when a man carries such an atmosphere around with him and gives its quality to all that he does and communicates its spirit to all who cross his path. This was the most remarkable impact of the life of the Master upon those whom he encountered. It was this that stilled the raging of the madman, that called little children to Him, that made sinners know that their sins were forgiven. His whole countenance glowed with the glory of the Father. And the secret? "A great while before day, he withdrew to a solitary place and prayed, as was his custom."

BIBLICAL WISDOM

In the morning, while it was still very dark, he got up and went out to a deserted place, and there he prayed. Mark 1:35

SILENCE FOR MEDITATION

QUESTIONS TO PONDER

- Jesus made a habit of withdrawing, of retreating, of going to be alone with God. How did it help him? How might it help you?
- Thurman writes that "the experience of prayer can be nurtured and cultivated." In what ways does your community of faith help to nurture and cultivate the practice of prayer? Is it enough?
- What is your habit of retreating and returning? Thurman suggests that we need a balance between times of prayer and times of action. What would such a balance look like?

Psalm Fragment

Give ear to my words, O Lord;
give heed to my sighing.
Listen to the sound of my cry,
my King and my God,
for to you I pray.
O Lord, in the morning you hear my voice;
in the morning I plead my case to you, and watch. Psalm 5:1-3

Journal Reflections

- In what ways (and by whom) has prayer been nurtured and cultivated in your life?
- Are you happy with your prayer life? Why or why not?
- Thurman says that prayer can become "a way of living" for an individual. What exactly do you think he means? Is prayer your way of living? Why or why not?

Prayers of Hope & Healing

Pray for those who don't know how (or don't bother) to speak with God, that they may discover the delights of conversation with the divine.

Prayer for Today

Throughout the day, O God, let me take the time to talk to you about my hopes and dreams, fears and struggles. Amen.

Notes

Journey

Day 21

THERE IS A MEDLEY OF confusion as to the meaning of personal freedom. For some it means to function without limitations at any point, to be able to do what one wants to do and without hindrance. This is the fantasy of many minds, particularly those that are young. For others, personal freedom is to be let alone, to be protected against any force that may move into their life with a swift and decisive imperative. For still others, it means to be limited in one's power over others only by one's own strength, energy, and perseverance.

The meaning of personal freedom is found in none of these. They lack the precious ingredient, the core of discipline and inner structure without which personal freedom is a delusion. At the very center personal freedom is a discipline of the mind and of the emotions. The mind must be centered upon a goal, a purpose, a plan. Of all possible goals, purposes, plans, a single one is lifted above the others and held as one's chosen direction. Then the individual knows when he is lost, when he has missed the way. There emerges a principle of orderedness, which becomes a guide for behavior and action. Under the circumstances, goals may be changed deliberately and the sense of random, pointless living is removed.

◞

BIBLICAL WISDOM

For freedom Christ has set us free. Stand firm, therefore, and do not submit again to a yoke of slavery. Galatians 5:1

SILENCE FOR MEDITATION

QUESTIONS TO PONDER

- In what ways does our culture define "freedom?"
- How do cultural definitions of freedom and Thurman's definition of freedom differ? Which do you think is correct? Why?

- In what ways does your community of faith encourage (or discourage) the exercise of personal freedom?

PSALM FRAGMENT

Who are they that fear the LORD?
He will teach them the way that they should choose. Psalm 25:12

JOURNAL REFLECTIONS

- Do you experience yourself as someone with "personal freedom"? Why or why not?
- Make a list of your personal goals, goals you have chosen for yourself.
- Reflect on your personal goals. In what ways are they connected to your faith?

PRAYERS OF HOPE & HEALING

Pray for those whose "freedom" is really a form of slavery, that they might experience the freedom in Christ to choose a life that is truly good for themselves and good for others.

PRAYER FOR TODAY

Liberating God, let me live each moment of this day in the freedom for which Christ has set me free. Amen.

NOTES

Day 22

SUCH A PRINCIPLE OF ORDEREDNESS provides a channel for one's emotions and drive. Energy is no longer dissipated but is used to supply dynamic for the pursuit of the end. Here we come upon the most interesting aspect of personal freedom—the living of one's life with confidence that transcends discouragement and despair. This means that one does not have to depend upon the favorable circumstance, the fortuitous "break," the applause, approval, and felicitation of friends, important as these are. The secret is the quiet inner purpose and the release of vitality with which it inspires the act. Achieving the goal is not measured by some external standard, though such must not be completely ignored. Rather, it is measured in terms of loyalty to the purpose and the freedom which it inspires.

"Seek ye first the rule of God," the Master says. And after that? The key that one needs for one's peace is in the heart. There can be no personal freedom where there is not an initial personal surrender.

~

BIBLICAL WISDOM

And whatever you do, in word or deed, do everything in the name of the Lord Jesus, giving thanks to God the Father through him. Colossians 3:17

SILENCE FOR MEDITATION

QUESTIONS TO PONDER

- How does choosing goals through the exercise of personal freedom give "orderedness" to our lives?
- Reflect on the ways in which consciously choosing positive goals "provides a channel for one's emotions and drive."
- What does it say about us if we refuse to organize ourselves by the strong use of our individual freedom to make choices?

PSALM FRAGMENT

As a deer longs for flowing streams,
*   so my soul longs for you, O God.*
My soul thirsts for God,
*   for the living God.* Psalm 42:1-2b

JOURNAL REFLECTIONS

- Write about what you think Thurman meant when he wrote: "The key that one needs for one's peace is in the heart." Do you hold that "key"?
- Do you agree with Thurman that "There can be no personal freedom where there is not an initial personal surrender"? Why or why not? To what (or to whom) should we surrender; and how do we do that?
- If you have had such an experience, write about "the quiet inner purpose and the release of vitality" that accompanied your pursuit of a freely chosen goal.

PRAYERS OF HOPE & HEALING

Pray for those whose lives are disordered, fragmented, aimless, that they might surrender themselves to the loving embrace of God and choose God's way as the goal of their lives.

PRAYER FOR TODAY

Loving God, for flowing streams, I pray; may they flow towards you and away from the desert of being confused, disoriented, disordered. Amen.

NOTES

Day 23

"A GREAT WHILE BEFORE DAY," says the book—the night was long and wearisome because the day had been full of jabbing annoyances; the high resolve of some winged moment had spent itself, no longer sure, no longer free, and then vanished as if it had never been; the need, the utter urgency was for some fresh assurance, the healing touch of a heavenly wing—"a great while before the day" he found his way to the quiet place in the hills. And prayed.

BIBLICAL WISDOM

Then Jesus told them a parable about their need to pray always and not to lose heart. Luke 18:1

SILENCE FOR MEDITATION

QUESTIONS TO PONDER

- In what ways does faith help you to contend with the "jabbing annoyances" of the day?
- In what ways might a community of faith bring "the healing touch of a heavenly wing" for people whose "high resolve" has dissipated?
- What do you do when your resolve "has spent itself" and "vanished as if it had never been"? Any other ways you might respond?

PSALM FRAGMENT

I lift up my eyes to the hills—
    from where will my help come?
My help comes from the LORD,
    who made heaven and earth. Psalm 121:1-2

Journal Reflections

- If you have a "quiet place in the hills" to be alone with God, describe it in your journal. If not, how might you find such a place?
- Make a list of the present "jabbing annoyances" of your day. Write about the way these daily annoyances interfere with both your personal goals and your relationship with God.
- Make a list of the people in your life who are able to bring you "the healing touch of a heavenly wing" when you need it. In what ways do you bring that healing touch to others?

Prayers of Hope & Healing

Pray for those who are disappointed or discouraged or in fear of failure, that they might receive "the healing touch of a heavenly wing."

Prayer for Today

Holy God, let me resolve this day to follow you in every way I can, and to seek from you the strength and wisdom to keep my resolve. Amen.

Notes

Journey

Day 24

SOMETHING FAR MORE PROFOUND IS at work. It is akin to adoration; it is the sheer joy in thanksgiving that God is God and the soul is privileged and blessed with the overwhelming consciousness of this. It is the kind of thanksgiving that sings itself to the Lord because He is God. This praiseful thanksgiving overshadows any bill of particulars, even though many particular things crowd into mind. We can get some notion of what is meant here when, under some circumstances, we encounter a person who, for what seems to be a swirling temporary moment, enjoys us—not what we say or what we are doing or what we represent, but who reaches into the core of our being and touches us purely. How such moments must rejoice the heart of God! I agree most heartily with Rufus Jones when he said that prayer at its best is when the soul enjoys God and prays out of sheer love of Him.

⁓

BIBLICAL WISDOM

Yet I will rejoice in the LORD;
I will exult in the God of my salvation.
GOD, the Lord, is my strength. . . . Habakkuk 3:18-19b

SILENCE FOR MEDITATION

QUESTIONS TO PONDER

- Is "adoration" a word that describes the tone of worship in your community of faith? Why or why not?
- What is the distinction between praying out of need and praying "out of sheer love" for God?
- In what ways does our delight in another person (or their delight in us) work as a metaphor for our relationship with God?

PSALM FRAGMENT

I will praise the name of God with a song;
I will magnify him with thanksgiving. Psalm 69:30

JOURNAL REFLECTIONS

- Make a list of what (and who) you are thankful for. After each entry in your list write the reasons for your thankfulness. Anything to learn from your list?
- Write about a time when someone simply enjoyed you, not because of what you say or do or represent, but because of who you are as a person. How did it feel?
- Write about a time when you simply enjoyed another person, not because of what they say or do or represent, but because of who they are as a person. How did it feel?

PRAYER OF HOPE & HEALING

Pray for those who could use a little joy in their lives, that they might delight in themselves, in others and in God.

PRAYER FOR TODAY

God of great delight, lift my feet off the ground today, lift my spirits, and teach me to rejoice. Amen.

NOTES

Journey

Day 25

IT HAS ALWAYS SEEMED CURIOUS to me that man should investigate the external world, recognize its order, and make certain generalizations about its behavior which he calls laws; that he should study his own organism and discover there a sort of orderliness of inner behavior, which he seeks to correct when it acts out of character by a wide variety of ministrations, from drugs and surgery to hypnosis and faith—and yet that he should be inclined at the same time, to regard himself as an entity apart from all the rest of creation, including his body. Man is body, but more than body; moreover, he is spirit. Therefore, it is not surprising that in man's spirit should be found the crucial nexus that connects him with the Creator of Life, the Spirit of the Living God. The apostle is utterly realistic when he says that in Him we live and move and have our being. The most natural thing in the world for man, then, would be to keep open the lines of communication between him and the Source of his life, out of which he comes and into which (it is my faith) he goes.

～

BIBLICAL WISDOM

Do you not know that you are God's temple and that God's Spirit dwells in you? 1 Corinthians 3:16

SILENCE FOR MEDITATION

QUESTIONS TO PONDER

- Does your community of faith stress the otherness and transcendence of God or the innerness and immanence of God? Or is there a balance between the otherness and innerness of God? Explain.
- The "lines of communication" that Thurman speaks of are the many kinds of prayer. Does your community of faith help you keep the lines of communication open?
- In what ways does our culture treat people as bodies? As spirits? As both?

PSALM FRAGMENT

By day the LORD commands his steadfast love,
and at night his song is with me,
a prayer to the God of my life. Psalm 42:8

JOURNAL REFLECTIONS

- In what ways, if any, have you experienced the innerness of God?
- Do you feel apart from or one with the creation and its creator? Explain.
- Are the "lines of communication" between you and the source of your life open or closed? Explain.

PRAYER OF HOPE & HEALING

Pray for those who do not experience themselves as the temple of God, that they might open to the indwelling, transforming, loving, guiding presence of God's Spirit.

PRAYER FOR TODAY

Listening God, when I pray let me have the grace to listen as much if not more than I speak. Amen.

NOTES

THE ORDER IN CREATION AND the orderly disorder that seem to characterize what is regarded as random activity in certain aspects of the world external to man, the concepts in the mind that are derivatives of man's experience with his senses, and those other concepts that seem to take their form from the boundless ebb and flow of the imageless tides that wash the shores of the human mind and spirit—all these express an authentic creativity that is Mind at work, and man is an essential part of the order. What is observed as a structure of orderliness or dependability in any and all expressions of life, from the simplest forms to the most complex, is seen most dramatically in the ability of man to create, to conceptualize, to plan, to function purposefully, and to implement in time and space what is idea or thought to the mind. . . . In man's experience with life, within him at all levels and about him in varied manifestations in time-space intervals, he is a part of the world of facts and meaning, suggesting creative intent. It seems reasonable, then, to assume that wherever life is found, evidence of creative intent must also exist in that which is being experienced, reacted to, observed, or studied. One such sign, and the most crucial one, is the way life seeks always to realize itself in wholeness, harmony, and integration within the potential that characterizes the particular expression of life. The most natural question that comes to mind, therefore, is: How did life get started? What was the beginning of it all?"

BIBLICAL WISDOM

In the beginning when God created the heavens and the earth the earth, was a formless void and darkness covered the face of the deep, while a wind from God swept over the face of the waters. Then God said, "Let there be light"; and there was light. And God saw that the light was good; and God separated the light from the darkness. God called the light Day, and the darkness he called Night. And there was evening and there was morning, the first day. Genesis 1:1-5

Silence for Meditation

Questions to Ponder

- Do you agree with Thurman that "wherever life is found, evidence of creative intent (God) must also exist in that which is being experienced, reacted to, observed, or studied"? Why or why not?
- What is the relationship between God's creativity and human creativity?
- Are we most human when we create? Explain.

Psalm Fragment

The heavens are telling the glory of God;
*   and the firmament proclaims his handiwork.*
Day to day pours forth speech,
*   and night to night declares knowledge.* Psalm 19:1-2

Journal Reflections

- Write your own answer to Thurman's question: "How did life get started? What was the beginning of it all?"
- Would you consider yourself a nature mystic—someone who experiences God in nature? Explain.
- Write about ways in which you are a creative person. In what ways does your creativity relate to your spirituality?

Prayers of Hope & Healing

Pray that all people might see the hand of the creator in the creation that we might all come to reverence all life and care for the world God made and loves.

Prayer for Today

Creating God, help me to discover and use the creative gifts you have given me and, in so doing, to bring joy and life to me and to the world you love. Amen.

Notes

Journey

Day 27

IT IS THIS INNER EQUILIBRIUM that must be maintained at all costs so that the person will stand ever in immediate candidacy for the direct visitation of God. This is the heart of the meaning of discipline in the religion of the mystic. All the negative things are present in the discipline, yes, this cannot be denied; the highly abnormal aberrations of mind are present, oftentimes, to be sure. But there is something more, there is strength, power released in the life of man here, a kind of concomitant overflowing of creative energies which demand that he be *true* himself by the highest. This he seeks to do through discipline with unrelenting austerity; he must bring himself, his will, his feelings, his very thoughts and impulses under the synthesizing scrutiny of God. All else is trivial and in a sense irrelevant. The greatest mystic-ascetics in the Christian tradition have turned the whole stream of Christian thought and achievement into new and powerful channels of practical living.

The flesh does fight against the spirit. In Jesus Christ as symbol . . . the Christian mystic sees the meaning of the triumph of the spirit over the body; the transcending and triumphant power of God over the most relentless pressure and persistence of things that divide and destroy. To know Him in the fellowship of His suffering seemed to the Christian mystic the key to his victory. In this the mystic proves himself a man of rarest insight and power. In this insight the mystic anticipates the needs of all men. We want deliverance from things which divide, which bind and render us impotent and purposeless. We want to find a controlling purpose for our lives. With relentlessness and fever we seek always to find meaning, in some ultimate sense, for our lives so that we may be able to live with dignity and courage in our world. This the mystic achieves by what to him is an experience of an absolute good and his ethical task is to retain that good in the "*for instances*" of experience.

BIBLICAL WISDOM

For those who live according to the flesh set their minds on the things of the flesh, but those who live according to the Spirit set their minds on the things of the Spirit. Romans 8:5

Silence for Meditation

Questions to Ponder

- How would you describe the difference between the flesh and the spirit?
- What do you think the words "mysticism" and "mystic" mean?
- Thurman advocates a spiritual discipline in which a person "must bring himself, his will, his feelings, his very thoughts and impulses under the synthesizing scrutiny of God." What do you think he means?

Psalm Fragment

O taste and see that the Lord is good;
    happy are those who take refuge in him. Psalm 34:8

Journal Reflections

- Do you consider yourself a mystic? If yes, describe your mystical experiences in your journal.
- What does it mean to you "to live with dignity and courage in our world"?
- Do you have the "inner equilibrium" or balance, or stability" which Thurman says is necessary for "the direct visitation of God"? Explain.

Prayers for Hope & Healing

Pray for all who seem to have lost equilibrium, that they might learn to balance flesh and spirit and so open themselves to the experience of God.

Prayer for Today

Holy God, grant me a taste of mysticism so that I may learn to order and manage my life in ways that open me to your presence. Amen.

Notes

Journey

Day 28

BETWEEN THE PRESENT ORDER OF society and that order of society which we have described is a perilous way but it is a way in which the affirmation mystic must chart his course. What then is his course of action? Let me gather up the threads of my position to this point: the affirmation mystic interprets the meaning of man's life in terms of an experienced unity with God in a conscious sense. "To know that our being has been taken up and made an organic part of His very self, because He wills and because we will it, is the end of true mysticism." What he experiences he is under obligation to achieve in experience. In his effort to achieve this in experience he is brought face to face with evil in his own life and in the lives of others and the reflection of this evil in the relationships by which he is bound to his fellows and his fellows are bound to him. He cannot escape the responsibility of working out the good in a manifold of inner and outer relations. He knows that he cannot escape in mere asceticism even as he recognizes its merits; he must embrace the social whole and seek to achieve empirically the good which has possessed him in his moment of profoundest insight. In his effort to do this, he constantly checks his action by his insight. It keeps his insight true and his action valid.

~

BIBLICAL WISDOM

Do you not know that your body is a temple of the Holy Spirit within you, which you have from God, and that you are not your own? I Corinthians 6:19

SILENCE FOR MEDITATION

QUESTIONS TO PONDER

- What does it mean to say that if you experience a mystical vision of unity with God you are then obligated to achieve that unity in daily experience?
- Why is it that when mystics try to express their spiritual experience of unity with God in their daily lives they are "brought face to face with evil" in their own lives and in the lives of others?

- Is mysticism false if it doesn't lead to positive social action? Why or why not?

PSALM FRAGMENT

Do not, O LORD, withhold
  your mercy from me;
  let your steadfast love and your faithfulness
  keep me safe forever.
For evils have encompassed me
  without number;
  my iniquities have overtaken me,
  until I cannot see. . . . Psalm 40:11-12a.

JOURNAL REFLECTIONS

- Thurman speaks of "affirmation mystics," people who seek to work out in social action the insights gained from their experience of unity with God. Would you consider yourself an "affirmation mystic"? Why or why not?
- Write about the relationship between your spirituality and social action.
- Write about a time when your spiritual experience confronted you with the reality of evil in yourself and in others.

PRAYERS OF HOPE & HEALING

Pray for people whose lives show a passion for social justice, that they might be strengthened, comforted, and encouraged by the vision of God.

PRAYER FOR TODAY

Grant me days filled with actions, O God, and nights awash in vision. Grant me a true openness to the power of your spirit in my everyday life. Amen.

NOTES

Day 29

CURIOUS INDEED IS THE FACT that at a time of crisis men must be constantly reminded that the crisis does not mark the end of all things. It is of the nature of crisis so to dominate the horizon of men's thoughts that everything that is not directly related to the crisis situation seems irrelevant and without significance. At such times men seem to accept the contradictions of experience as being in themselves ultimate. The crisis throws everything out of proportion, out of balance and the balance seems always superficially to be on the side of disaster, on the side of negation. . . . If the contradictions of experience are ultimate, then the conflict between right and wrong, good and evil, order and chaos can never be resolved and human life is caught eternally in the agonizing grip of a firm and eternal struggle between these two forces. But such a dualism has never been able to satisfy the deepest searchings of the mind and the heart of man. The human spirit at long last is not willing to accept the contradiction of life as being ultimate. There continues ever a margin on the side of the good—yes, the ultimate destiny of man is good—this affirmation becomes the ground of optimism and inspiration in the bitterest crisis when times are "out of joint," when men have lost their reason and sitting in the "sepulchers of gloom watch their dreams go silently to dust." It is the peculiar task of the preacher to recognize this deep urge within man and to call it to bear witness at all times, but particularly at such a moment as is our own (World War II), now that the whole round world is rolling in darkness.

~

BIBLICAL WISDOM

We are afflicted in every way, but not crushed; perplexed, but not driven to despair; persecuted, but not forsaken; struck down, but not destroyed; always carrying in the body the death of Jesus, so that the life of Jesus may also be made visible in our bodies. 2 Corinthians 4:8-10

Silence for Meditation

Questions to Ponder

- In what ways does your community of faith help its people deal with crisis?
- Do you agree with Thurman that "the ultimate destiny" of humankind is good? Why or why not?
- Does God disappear when times are out of joint or is God ever more present? Explain.

Psalm Fragment

The LORD is a stronghold for the oppressed,
*   a stronghold in times of trouble.*
And those who know your name put their trust in you,
*   for you, O LORD, have not forsaken those who seek you.* Psalm 9:9-10

Journal Reflections

- When you find yourself in times of trouble do you tend to rely on your own strength or do you seek help from others? From God?
- Write about a time of crisis in your life. What inner and external resources were available to you? What did you learn from the experience? Where was God in your experience of crisis?
- Have you ever watched a dream "go silently to dust"? If yes, how did you respond? If no, how do you imagine you would respond to such an experience?

Prayers of Hope & Healing

Pray for those whose dreams have gone "silently to dust," that out of the dust may come new hope, new promise, new dreams.

Prayer for Today

Ever-present God, give me the wisdom and the memory to know that in times of trouble I am not alone for you are with me. Amen.

Notes

Journey

Day 30

THE STRENGTH OF THE PERSONAL life is often found in the depth and intensity of its isolation. The fight for selfhood is unending. There is the ever-present need to stand alone, unsupported and unchallenged. To be sure of one's self, to be counted for one's self *as* one's self, is to experience aliveness in its most exciting dimension. If there is a job of work to be done that is impossible, if there is a need to be met that is limitless, if there is a word to be said that can never be said, the spirit of the whole man is mustered and in the exhaustive effort he finds *himself* in the solitariness of strength renewed and courage regained. Below the surface of all the activity and functioning in which life engages us, there is a level of disengagement when the individual is a private actor on a lonely stage. It is here that things are seen without their outer garbs—the seedlings of desires take quiet root, the bitter waters and the sweet springs find their beginnings, the tiny stirrings that become the raging tempests are seen to shimmer in the semi-darkness—this "the region," "the place," "the clime" where man is the lonely solitary guest in the vast empty house of the world.

~

BIBLICAL WISDOM

So we do not lose heart. Even though our outer nature is wasting away, our inner nature is being renewed day by day. For this slight momentary affliction is preparing us for an eternal weight of glory beyond all measure, because we look not at what can be seen but at what cannot be seen; for what can be seen is temporary, but what cannot be seen is eternal. 2 Corinthians 4:16-18

SILENCE FOR MEDITATION

QUESTIONS TO PONDER

- Do you agree with Thurman that "the strength of the personal life is often found in the depth and intensity of its isolation"? Why or why not?

- What is the relationship between individuality and community?
- Thurman states that the "fight for selfhood is unending." What is "selfhood"? How do you carry on the "fight for selfhood"?

PSALM FRAGMENT

O LORD, you have searched me and known me.
You know when I sit down and when I rise up;
*   you discern my thoughts from far away.*
You search out my path and my lying down,
*   and are acquainted with all my ways.* Psalm 139:1-3

JOURNAL REFLECTIONS

- Are you comfortable with solitude? Do you have a good balance in your life between time alone and time with others? Explain.
- Thurman states: "To be sure of one's self, to be counted for one's self *as* one's self, is to experience aliveness in its most exciting dimension." Do you resonate with Thurman's assertion? Why or why not?
- What obstacles have you encountered in your own "fight for selfhood"? What encouragement and successes have you experienced?

PRAYERS OF HOPE & HEALING

Pray for those who are too solitary, that they may discover the joy of community. Pray for those who are too surrounded by others, that they may discover the joy of solitude.

PRAYER FOR TODAY

Holy God, let me get the balance right between solitude and community so I might be good for myself and good for others as well.

NOTES

Day 31

FOR THE MOST PART, NEGRO churches in America have been built by the pennies, nickels, and dimes of simple toilers. For this reason, if for no other, there is a sense of possession which they feel for the church which is unique. As an old lady said to a passerby as she stood weeping because her church was being burned: "I wouldn't mind it, son, but that's blood money that's being burned."

~

BIBLICAL WISDOM

He sat down opposite the treasury, and watched the crowd putting money into the treasury. Many rich people put in large sums. A poor widow came and put in two small copper coins, which are worth a penny. Then he called his disciples and said to them, "Truly I tell you, this poor widow has put in more than all those who are contributing to the treasury. For all of them have contributed out of their abundance; but she out of her poverty has put in everything she had, all she had to live on." Mark 12:41-44

SILENCE FOR MEDITATION

QUESTIONS TO PONDER

- How committed do you feel to your community of faith? How is that commitment expressed?
- How common do you think it is for people to have "sweat equity" (or as the woman in today's reading, "blood equity") in their church? Explain.
- What does stewardship mean to the rich? What does it mean to the poor?

PSALM FRAGMENT

It is zeal for your house that has consumed me;
the insults of those who insult you have fallen on me. Psalm 66:9

Journal Reflections

- In your journal, evaluate your stewardship—the giving of your time, talents, and money to support your community of faith.
- Make a list of the organizations in which you have sweat equity. What makes them that important to you?
- Write about how you understand the relationship between faith and stewardship.

Prayers of Hope & Healing

Offer a prayer of thanksgiving for those who, having little, support the life and ministry of their faith community. Offer a prayer of forgiveness for those who, having much, fail to do all they could to support the life and ministry of their faith community.

Prayer for Today

God of great generosity, help me to use my many gifts and means in the service of your church and your people. Amen.

Notes

Day 32

A DYNAMIC IDEA CANNOT CONTINUE to persist unless it is housed in some form of organization. In order for it to become intelligible it must be couched in current concepts and the like. The disciples of Jesus were not long in discovering this fact. (It has always impressed me that Jesus did not seem to make the same discovery unless we think of his disciples as a form of organization. They were more of a fellowship.) It is also true that just as a dynamic idea is consecrated in some form of organization, it is also destroyed by the very organization that preserved it. Hence the paradox: The power that makes it breaks it. The minister must encourage the development of systematic procedure in the institutional religious life but it must be clear to him and he must make it clear to his people that the Spirit of Jesus grows by contagion and not by organization. One life aglow with the Spirit of Jesus is far more efficacious than a dozen organizational attempts to salvage society. In the final analysis a man's life is changed by contact with another life.

⌒

BIBLICAL WISDOM

Let no one despise your youth, but set the believers an example in speech and conduct, in love, in faith, in purity. . . . Pay close attention to yourself and to your teaching; continue in these things, for in doing this you will save both yourself and your hearers. 1 Timothy 4:12, 16

SILENCE FOR MEDITATION

QUESTIONS TO PONDER

• What did Thurman mean when he wrote that "just as a dynamic idea is consecrated in some form of organization, it is also destroyed by the very organization that preserved it"?

- How can a religious organization stay more like a fellowship or movement and less like an organization or institution?
- Do you agree that the "Spirit of Jesus grows by contagion and not by organization"? Why or why not?

PSALM FRAGMENT

We ponder your steadfast love, O God,
in the midst of your temple. Psalm 48:9

JOURNAL REFLECTIONS

- Write about how your life has been changed by "contact with another life."
- Write about how someone else's life was changed by contact with your life.
- Make a list of the ways the organized church is faithful to the ideas that come from Jesus' teaching. Make a list of the ways the church is unfaithful to those ideas.

PRAYERS OF HOPE & HEALING

Pray for all those who have been disappointed or burnt by religious organizations, that they may discover the beautiful teaching that gave birth to those organizations and be healed.

PRAYER FOR TODAY

Great God of love, let me learn of love in your house and live love in your world. Amen.

NOTES

Journey

Day 33

THE NEGRO MINISTER MUST FIND how to interpret life in terms of a creative expansive idealism. Therefore he must be a student. For instance, he must know what the problem of evolution is and must be prepared to think clear through it with the anxious ones who share their doubts with him. He must be aware of the findings in all the major fields of human knowledge and interpret their meaning in terms of the Kingdom of God.

He must be a thinker. He must sense the dilemmas which his people face in American life and must offer intelligent spiritual and practical guidance to them. To his eye must be clear the thin line between cowardice and fear and dynamic redemptive love. He must judge the ethical significance of the religion of Jesus in the light of the Zulu proverb: "Full belly child says to empty belly child, be of good cheer."

He must be God-conscious. This will keep him close to life and will serve also as a valuational consciousness which will reveal the meaning of all the facts of experience. It will be to him a creative synthesis in the light of which all the facts of science or what not may be viewed.

~

BIBLICAL WISDOM

If a brother or sister is naked and lacks daily food, and one of you says to them, "Go in peace; keep warm and eat your fill," and yet you do not supply their bodily needs, what is the good of that? So faith by itself, if it has no works, is dead. James 2:15-17

SILENCE FOR MEDITATION

QUESTIONS TO PONDER

• What do you think Thurman meant when he pointed to the need to "interpret life in terms of a creative expansive idealism"? Why would this be important to African-American ministers? To any minister?

- In what way is the Zulu proverb—"Full belly child says to empty belly child, be of good cheer"—a good measure of the ethical relevance of Christianity?
- What is God-consciousness? How can it be cultivated?

PSALM FRAGMENT

Happy are those who consider the poor;
the LORD delivers them in the day of trouble. Psalm 41:1

JOURNAL REFLECTIONS

- Would you describe your view of life in terms of idealism, or realism, or cynicism? Explain.
- To what degree do you think you have a "God-consciousness"? Explain. Is there anything you could do to cultivate a greater God-consciousness?
- Write about the ways in which your faith moves you to works of charity and justice.

PRAYERS OF HOPE & HEALING

Pray for all pastors and other leaders in the church, that from their consciousness of God they would provide strong spiritual and ethical leadership.

PRAYER FOR TODAY

God of all wisdom, grant me wisdom through the teaching, preaching, and mentoring of wise leaders of your church. Amen.

NOTES

Journey

Day 34

DESPITE ALL THAT HAS BEEN said about the pattern of segregation in our society, it is my conviction that time is against it. In fact, much of the current effort to hold the line may be viewed as a back-against-the-wall endeavor. The more the world becomes a neighborhood in which time and space are approaching zero as a limit, the more urgent becomes the issue of neighborliness. Man can now circle the entire earth's surface in a matter of minutes. Communication is now instant! This means that the external symbols of segregation—the wall, the ghetto, the separate locale as a mandatory restriction binding upon groups of people because of race, color, creed, or national origin—cannot survive modern life. The emphasis here is upon the two words "external symbols." When I suggest that time is against the pattern of segregation, I am referring to the symbols. The walls are crumbling—this is one of the dramatic facts of our world. The fact itself is very frightening to many who have lived always behind the walls, within the walls, or beyond the walls. It is deeply disturbing also to those who have found the existence of the walls essential to their own peace, well-being, and security. Out of sight, out of mind—this can no longer be the case.

BIBLICAL WISDOM

For he is our peace; in his flesh he has made both groups into one and has broken down the dividing wall, that is, the hostility between us. Ephesians 2:14

SILENCE FOR MEDITATION

QUESTIONS TO PONDER

- Thurman wrote this piece in the 1960s. Was he right when he said "the walls are crumbling"? Why or why not?
- Why is the crumbling of the walls "frightening to many who have lived always behind the walls, within the walls, or beyond the walls"?

- How might the church fight the "out of sight, out of mind" mindset with respect to the plight of the discriminated against?

PSALM FRAGMENT

May he defend the cause of the poor of the people,
give deliverance to the needy,
and crush the oppressor. Psalm 72:4

JOURNAL REFLECTIONS

- Journal about your present understanding of the relations between Blacks and Whites in America.
- Make a list of the people groups who are discriminated against in our country. Are you a member of any of these groups? If so, describe your experience of being "behind the wall."
- Write about ways you participate (or could participate) in dismantling the many walls that separate people in our society.

PRAYERS OF HOPE & HEALING

Pray for all people, especially children, whose lives are diminished by "walls," that the walls that constrain them might crumble.

PRAYER FOR TODAY

God and creator of all people, today let me be about the business of tearing down the walls that divide. Amen.

NOTES

Journey

Day 35

THIS IS THE IDEA. A man can send his imagination forth to establish a beachhead in another man's spirit, and from that vantage point so to blend with the other's landscape that what he sees and feels is authentic—this is the great adventure in human relations. But this is not enough. The imagination must report its findings accurately without regard to prejudgments and private or collective fears. But this too is not enough. There must be both a spontaneous and a calculating response to such knowledge which will result in sharing of life and resources at their deepest level.

This is to experience oneself as a human being and to have that essential experience illumined and underscored by experiencing one's fellows as human beings. This is what every person seeks to have happen to himself. Every man lives under the necessity for being at home in his own house, as it were. He must not seem to himself to be alien to himself. This is the thing that happens when other human beings relate to him as if he were not a human being or less than a human being. It is possible for a man to declassify whole groups of people on the basis of certain criteria which he establishes or which he inherits. For instance, it may be to denigrate all people who come from a particular country, locale, or region, or all who speak a certain language, or all whose skin has pigmentation of any kind or a particular kind, or all who claim a different religious faith.

BIBLICAL WISDOM

There is no longer Jew or Greek, there is no longer slave or free, there is no longer male and female; for all of you are one in Christ Jesus. Galatians 3:28

SILENCE FOR MEDITATION

QUESTIONS TO PONDER

- What does Thurman mean by establishing "a beachhead" in another person's spirit?
- Why is it so difficult to have empathy for people who are different from us?
- What does it mean to be at home in your own house?

PSALM FRAGMENT

I cry to you, O LORD;
I say, "You are my refuge,
my portion in the land of the living." Psalm 142:5

JOURNAL REFLECTIONS

- Write about a time when you were able to "establish a beachhead" in another person's spirit. What did you learn?
- Are you at home in your own house? Explain.
- Have you ever been persecuted because you were somehow different from the dominant group? Have you ever persecuted anyone because they were different? If yes, write about the experiences and what you have learned from them. If not, can you imagine such experiences?

PRAYERS OF HOPE & HEALING

Pray for those who are persecuted and pray for those who persecute, that there might be an end to racism, an end to thinking in color, an end to the divisions between people.

PRAYER FOR TODAY

God of oneness, use me today in some small but sure way to promote human community. Amen.

NOTES

Day 36

THE RELIGIOUS EXPERIENCE AS I have known it seems to swing wide the door, not merely into Life but into lives. I am confident that my own call to the religious vocation cannot be separated from the slowly emerging disclosure that my religious experience makes it possible for me to experience myself as a human being and thus keep a very real psychological distance between myself and the hostilities of my environment. Through the years it has driven me more and more to seek to make as a normal part of my relations with men the experiencing of them as human beings. When this happens love has essential materials with which to work. And contrary to the general religious teaching, men would not need to stretch themselves out of shape in order to love. On the contrary, a man comes into possession of himself more completely when he is free to love another.

⁓

BIBLICAL WISDOM

Owe no one anything, except to love one another; for the one who loves another has fulfilled the law. Romans 13:8

SILENCE FOR MEDITATION

QUESTIONS TO PONDER

- How does religious experience make it possible for us to experience ourselves as a human being?
- What does it mean to experience others as human beings?
- What does it mean to keep a psychological distance between yourself and the hostilities of your environment? How does religious experience assist in maintaining that distance?

Psalm Fragment

When I look at your heavens, the work of your fingers,
the moon and the stars that you have established;
what are human beings that you are mindful of them,
mortals that you care for them?
Yet you have made them a little lower than God,
and crowned them with glory and honor. Psalm 8:3-5

Journal Reflections

- Has your religious experience opened you to the lives of others? If so, how? If not, why not?
- Do you experience yourself as someone who is free to love? Why or why not?
- Thurman writes that people come into possession of themselves more completely when they are free to love another. Has that been your experience? If so, describe the experience. If not, can you imagine such an experience?

Prayers of Hope & Healing

Pray for those who seem not in complete possession of themselves, that they might experience the love that makes us truly human.

Prayer for Today

God of love, let me more and more deeply experience the capacity to love. Amen.

Notes

Journey

Day 37

ALL AROUND US WORLDS ARE dying and new worlds are being born; all around us life is dying and life is being born. The fruit ripens on the tree, the roots are silently at work in the darkness of the earth against a time when there shall be new leaves, fresh blossoms, green fruit. Such is the growing edge! It is the extra breath from the exhausted lung, the one more thing to try when all else has failed, the upward reach of life when weariness closes in upon all endeavor. This is the basis of hope in moments of despair, the incentive to carry on when times are out of joint and men have lost their reason, the source of confidence when worlds crash and dreams whiten into ash. The birth of the child—life's most dramatic answer to death—this is the growing edge incarnate. Look well to the growing edge!

~

BIBLICAL WISDOM

Look, the young woman is with child and shall bear a son, and shall name him Immanuel (God with us). Isaiah 7:14

SILENCE FOR MEDITATION

QUESTIONS TO PONDER

- Thurman believes that "the growing edge" is built into creation by the creator and is thus the "basis of hope," "the incentive to carry on," and "the source of confidence" as we experience the ups and downs of life. Do you agree? Why or why not?
- In what ways does your community of faith symbolize "the growing edge"?
- In what ways is the birth of the child—be it the Christ child or any child—"life's most dramatic answer to death"?

Psalm Fragment

O LORD, how manifold are your works!
  In wisdom you have made them all;
  the earth is full of your creatures. . . .
These all look to you
  to give them their food in due season;
  when you give to them, they gather it up;
  when you open your hand, they are filled with good things.
When you hide your face, they are dismayed;
  when you take away their breath, they die
  and return to their dust.
When you send forth your spirit, they are created;
  and you renew the face of the ground. Psalm 104:24, 27-30

Journal Reflections

• What experiences have you had of "the growing edge" in your own life?
• Write from the perspective of your personal faith about the place and
  meaning of death in creation.
• In terms of your daily life, what does it (or could it) mean to you to "look
  well to the growing edge"?

Prayers of Hope & Healing

Pray for all who are exhausted, who have lost hope and incentive and confidence; that they may be reinvigorated by tapping into the growing edge.

Prayer for Today

God who creates and sustains life and brings life out of death, today may I
"look well to the growing edge"! Amen.

Notes

Journey

Day 38

As a result of a series of fortuitous consequences there appeared on the horizon of the common life a young man who for a swift, staggering, and startling moment met the demands of the hero. He was young. He was well-educated with the full credentials of academic excellence in accordance with ideals found in white society. He was a son of the South. He was steeped in and nurtured by familiar religious tradition. He had charisma, that intangible quality of personality that gathers up in its magic the power to lift people out of themselves without diminishing them. In him the "outsider" and the "insider" came together in a triumphant synthesis. Here at last was a man who affirmed the oneness of black and white under a transcendent unity, for whom community meant the profoundest sharing in the common life. For him, the wall was a temporary separation between brothers. And his name was Martin Luther King, Jr. . . .

At last there was a available a personal and collective catharsis. . . . Never again would the boundaries be as established as they were before his coming. In his own short and intense life, the announcement was made to all and sundry, far and near, that the life of the black man was not at the mercy of the white man. That for better or worse they were tied together. No black man could be what his potential demanded unless the white man could be what *his* potential demanded. No white man could be what his potential demanded unless the black man could be what *his* potential demanded.

⌒

Biblical Wisdom

"You shall love the Lord your God with all your heart, and with all your soul, and with all your mind." This is the greatest and first commandment. And a second is like it: "You shall love your neighbor as yourself." On these two commandments hang all the law and the prophets. Matthew 22:37-40

Silence for Meditation

Questions to Ponder

- What does Thurman mean by the "transcendent unity" that leads us to affirm the "oneness of black and white"?
- To what degree and in what ways does your community of faith promote "the profoundest sharing in the common life" by diverse peoples?
- Should anyone's life be at the mercy of anyone else? Explain.

Psalm Fragment

I will sing of loyalty and of justice;
*   to you, O LORD, I will sing.*
I will study the way that is blameless.
When shall I attain it?
I will walk with integrity of heart. . . . Psalm 101:1-2

Journal Reflections

- In what ways might your life be at the mercy of others?
- In what ways might other peoples' lives be at your mercy?
- If there is "one God and Father of all, who is above all and through all and in all (Ephesians 4:6), can discrimination or oppression or exploitation of one by another ever be OK? Explain.

Prayers of Hope & Healing

Pray for all who share the vision of Martin Luther King, Jr., that they might have the courage and encouragement to stay the course in the struggle for an abundant common life from which no one is excluded.

Prayer for Today

God of no partiality, today let me look at those around me and see only brothers and sisters, beloved children of God. Amen.

Notes

Journey

Day 39

IT IS THE NATURE OF dreams to run riot, never to wish to contain themselves within limitations that are fixed. Sometimes they seem to be the cry of the heart for the boundless and the unexplored. Often they are fashioned out of longings too vital to die, out of hankerings fed by hidden springs in the dark places of the spirit. Often they are the offspring of hopes that can never be realized and longings that can never find fulfillment. Sometimes they are the weird stirrings of ghosts of dead plans and the kindling of ashes in a hearth that has long since been deserted. Many and fancy are the names by which dreams are called—fantasies, repressed desires, vanities of the spirit, will-of-the wisps. Sometimes we seek to dismiss them by calling their indulgence daydreaming, by which we mean taking flight from the realities of our own world and dwelling in the twilight of vain imaginings.

All of this may be true. But all their meaning need not be exhausted by such harsh judgment. The dreams belong to us; they come full-blown out of the real world in which we work and hope and carry on. They are not imposters. . . . No! Our dreams are our *thing*.

꙾

BIBLICAL WISDOM

I will pour out my spirit on all flesh;
your sons and your daughters shall prophesy,
your old men shall dream dreams,
and your young men shall see visions. Joel 2:28

SILENCE FOR MEDITATION

QUESTIONS TO PONDER

- What would it be like to have no dreams, no hopes, no goals?
- What does Thurman mean when he says our dreams for ourselves are not imposters, but rather that "our dreams are our *thing*"?

- What is the process by which dreams can be tested against reality? In what ways can our dreams for ourselves help to shape reality?

PSALM FRAGMENT

When the LORD restored the fortunes of Zion,
*   we were like those who dream.*
Then our mouth was filled with laughter,
*   and our tongue with shouts of joy. . . .* Psalm 120:1-2a

JOURNAL REFLECTIONS

- At this moment in your life what are your dreams? Are they realizable? What steps are you taking to realize them?
- Have you ever had dreams that are now no more than "the weird stirrings of ghosts of dead plans and the kindling of ashes in a hearth that has long since been deserted"? If so, describe them. What went wrong? Could (or should) these dreams be resurrected?
- In what sense could it be said of you: "My dreams are my thing"?

PRAYERS OF HOPE & HEALING

Pray for those who seem to have no dreams, no hopes, no goals, that they would catch the vision of a better, richer, more meaningful life for themselves and others.

PRAYER FOR TODAY

God of today and tomorrow, I pray for really good dreams; for dreams that inspire me and move me and shake me up. Amen.

NOTES

Journey

Day 40

FOR SOME MEN THERE CAN be no security in life apart from being surrounded by the broad expanse of country in which all landmarks are clear and the journey is along a well-worn path. Day after day they must be able to look up at any moment know exactly where they are. Their lives feed on the familiar tidbits concerning those to whom one long adjustment has been made, and the possibility of the sudden shift in temperament or behavior almost never occurs. There is a strange comfort in the assurance of the commonplace and familiar. Everything is in its place and all things are arranged in a neat pattern of stability. The one great fear is the fear of change; the one great dread is the dread of strangeness. . . .

[But Martin] Buber says that life for him is at its very best when he is living on what he calls "the narrow ridge." It is a way of life that generates zest for each day's round because it is lived in anticipation. . . . Each day's length is rimmed round with a margin of the joy of the unexpected, the anticipation of the new and the significant. . . . The accent, the bias, of such a life is on the side of the margin, the overtone, rather than a mere acceptance of the commonplace and the ordinary. If such is one's prevailing attitude, then even the commonplace becomes infused with the kind of vitality that gives it a new meaning.

⁓

BIBLICAL WISDOM

So if anyone is in Christ, there is a new creation: everything old has passed away; see, everything has become new! 2 Corinthians 5:17

SILENCE FOR MEDITATION

QUESTIONS TO PONDER

• There may be comfort, but can there be real joy when "everything is in its place and all things are arranged in a neat pattern of stability"? Explain.
• What would a life lived on the "narrow ridge" look like?

- Does your faith community encourage faith lived on the "narrow ridge" or faith lived "in the assurance of the commonplace and familiar"?

PSALM FRAGMENT

O sing to the LORD a new song;
*   sing to the LORD, all the earth.* Psalm 96:1

JOURNAL REFLECTIONS

- Are you a person who fears change and strangeness or does change and strangeness enliven and excite you? Explain.
- Does life lived on the "narrow ridge" describe your life? Why or why not?
- In what ways does your faith infuse even the commonplace and ordinary in your life with new meaning and vitality?

PRAYERS OF HOPE & HEALING

Pray for those who are stuck in patterns of behavior and daily routines that keep them from following God into new adventures, that they might open to the possibilities to be found in the unexpected and the unanticipated.

PRAYER FOR TODAY

Holy One, today and all days let me follow Jesus in the way of God no matter where it may take me. Amen.

NOTES

JOURNEY'S END

You have finished your *40-Day Journey with Howard Thurman*. I hope it has been a good journey and that along the way you have learned much, experienced much, and found good resources to deepen your faith and practice. As a result of this journey:

- How are you different?
- What have you learned?
- What have you experienced?
- In what ways has your faith and practice been transformed?

NOTES

For Further Reading

Books by Howard Thurman

The Centering Moment. Richmond, Indiana: Friends United Press, 1984.

Deep is the Hunger. Richmond, Indiana: Friends United Press, 1978.

Disciplines of the Spirit. Richmond, Indiana: Friends United Press, 1963.

The Creative Encounter. Richmond, Indiana: Friends United Press, 1972.

The Inward Journey. Richmond, Indiana: Friends United Press, 2007.

The Growing Edge. Richmond, Indiana: Friends United Press, 1974.

The Luminous Darkness. Richmond, Indiana: Friends United Press, 1989.

The Search For Common Ground. Richmond, Indiana: Friends United Press, 1986.

Temptations of Justice. Richmond, Indiana: United Friends Press, 1978.

With Head and Heart: The Autobiography of Howard Thurman. New York: Mariner Books, 1981.

Meditations of the Heart. Boston: Beacon Press, 1999.

Jesus and the Disinherited. Boston: Beacon Press, 1996.

An Anthology of Thurman's Work

A Strange Freedom: The Best of Howard Thurman on Religious Experience and Public Life, edited by Walter Earl Fluker and Catherine Tumber. Boston: Beacon Press, 1998.

Sources

(All readings were taken from *A Strange Freedom: The Best of Howard Thurman on Religious Experience and Public Life.* Reprinted by permission of Beacon Press, Boston.)

Day 1:   23   *Barren or Fruitful?*—A sermon from 1932
Day 2:   26   *Barren or Fruitful?*
Day 3:   28   *Barren or Fruitful?*
Day 4:   28   *Barren or Fruitful?*
Day 5:   80-81   *Disciplines of the Spirit*
Day 6:   81   *Disciplines of the Spirit*
Day 7:   132   *Jesus and the Disinherited*
Day 8:   56   *The Negro Spiritual Speaks of Life and Death*—
                 The Ingersoll Lecture, 1947
Day 9:   57   *The Negro Spiritual Speaks of Life and Death*
Day 10: 66-67   *The Negro Spiritual Speaks of Life and Death*
Day 11: 35-36   *Disciplines of the Spirit*
Day 12: 84   *Disciplines of the Spirit*
Day 13: 87-88   *Disciplines of the Spirit*
Day 14: 90   *Disciplines of the Spirit*
Day 15: 90-91   *Disciplines of the Spirit*
Day 16: 93   *Disciplines of the Spirit*
Day 17: 93-94   *Disciplines of the Spirit*
Day 18: 95   *Disciplines of the Spirit*
Day 19: 96   *Disciplines of the Spirit*
Day 20: 96   *Disciplines of the Spirit*
Day 21: 99   *The Inward Journey*
Day 22: 100   *The Inward Journey*
Day 23: 84   *Disciplines of the Spirit*

NOTES

NOTES

NOTES

NOTES